for Jack Anderson

&

in memory of Anna Frew

THE PURSUIT OF LEISURE
Victorian Depictions of Pastimes

Catalogue of an exhibition curated by
Gail-Nina Anderson and Joanne Wright

The Djanogly Art Gallery in association with Lund Humphries Publishers

DJANOGLY
artgallery

First Published in Great Britain in 1997 for the exhibition *The Pursuit of Leisure: Victorian Depictions of Pastimes*, by The Djanogly Art Gallery, University of Nottingham Arts Centre in association with Lund Humphries Publishers Limited, Park House, 1 Russell Gardens, London NW11 9NN.

Exhibition venues and dates:

The Djanogly Art Gallery
University of Nottingham Arts Centre
University Park, Nottingham
1 November – 14 December 1997

Royal Albert Memorial Museum
Queen Street, Exeter
27 December 1997 – 21 March 1998

British Library Cataloguing-in-Publication Data
A Catalogue record for this book is available from the British Library

Djanogly Art Gallery ISBN : 1 900809 35 4
Lund Humphries ISBN : 0 85331 761 5

Printed by Chas Goater & Son Ltd., Nottingham

Contents

Acknowledgements

The realisation of a project of this scale and variety depends on a great deal of goodwill, support and expert guidance. Our first acknowledgement must be of our enormous debt both to the institutions and to the private individuals who agreed to lend their works to the show and to those who then patiently dealt with our requests for information, photography and loan forms. Grateful thanks are also due to Christopher Wood who gave freely of his time and expert advice and to Elizabeth Prettejohn, Stephen Wildman and David Beevers who were all generous with their specialist knowledge. We received invaluable information about the history of cycling from Derek Roberts, and greatly refined our understanding of the rules of cricket through discussion with Peter Hurford, whilst Ann Hurford provided the support of friendship and regular hospitality which made our collaboration much easier than it might otherwise have been. Peter, Jessica and Miriam patiently tolerated the disruption of family life by fax, proof and phone.

The staff of the Djanogly Art Gallery has, as always, worked tirelessly to bring the exhibition into being. We must particularly thank the Exhibitions Secretary, Tracey Isgar, who has shouldered a huge administrative burden in the run up to the show, dealing with aspects of the preparation as various as transport, insurance and photographic credits. Our designer, David Bickerstaff of Johnston Bickerstaff and Jacqui Grafton of Chas Goater and Son, have worked together to produce this catalogue which, we feel sure, will continue to give pleasure, long after the exhibition is over.

Gail-Nina Anderson
Joanne Wright

THE PURSUIT OF LEISURE
Victorian Depictions of Pastimes

Gail-Nina Anderson

He said we should have fresh air, exercise and quiet; the constant change of scene would occupy our minds... and the hard work would give us a good appetite and make us sleep well.

Jerome K Jerome, *Three Men in a Boat*,1889

To judge from its pictorial art, Victorian Britain was anxious to envisage itself as a leisured society. Anxiety and leisure are odd bedfellows however, and the development and diversification of the 'leisure painting' signals an uneasy cross-fertilisation between modern life, contemporary art and artistic precedent.

Throughout Victoria's reign the Royal Academy maintained its status as the single most important art institution in Britain and many of the paintings in this catalogue were first shown on the walls of its annual Summer Exhibition. Academic authority, however, carried with it inevitable patterns of expectation against which new art could be measured, and one of these was generic categorisation. From the grand generalities of History Painting through the variable specificities of landscape, portrait and still-life, achievement was graded by reference to a preconceived relationship of style to its subject. The category where this was most fluid (and, predictably, the one which developed so freely during the nineteenth century as to challenge the whole system of classification) was that of 'genre painting', or scenes of everyday life. Always something of a catch-all term, during the eighteenth century this might have included anything from Hogarth's modern moral histories to sentimental little scenes of rustic dalliance. More relevant to Victorian taste, however, is the earlier precedent of Dutch seventeenth-century art. In Holland a newly-consolidated sense of national identity and a shift in economic demography led to an expanded art market wherein middle-class patronage promoted the production of pictures domestic both in scale and subject. Heroic classicism and religious iconography waned in favour of landscape, still-life, portraiture and images of the Dutch themselves. Suddenly, figures making music in an interior, skating on a frozen river or carousing in an inn constituted suffcient material for representation, without needing any literary or religious reference. That such imagery tended to be encoded with moral messages or social comment apparent to a contemporary audience scarcely needs stating, but this does not alter an evident delight in simply seeing their environments and activities mapped, explored and vicariously enjoyed through the process of representation.

A survey of Old Master sales and exhibitions demonstrates the popularity of Dutch art amongst Victorian collectors, and its direct impact on contemporary painting can be readily illustrated, as seen on the left. More generally, however, the nineteenth-century taste for the everyday developed not so much as a borrowing from seventeenth-century genre painting as from a parallel situation in the art markets of the two periods. Under Victoria there was a broader base for the enjoyment and acquisition of art than there had been in

The Duet.
George Adolphus Storey, 1869
Walker Art Gallery, Liverpool

the preceding century. The opening of public galleries, increased coverage in newspapers and specialised magazines and the growing sophistication of means of reproduction (including photography) all function both as the result of a burgeoning artistic awareness and as the means whereby it grew. The Old Masters were available for reappraisal, High Art was subject to regular adulatory revivals, classicism was re-invented, religious imagery was re-instated, but as a bedrock to these loftier concerns, there developed a massive market in Victorian pictures of Victorian life. The term 'genre painting' becomes too limiting for this effervescence of contemporary imagery, especially given the lively interaction of ideas between photography, graphic illustration and art. One must conclude that the Victorians wanted and needed to see their own society pictorially enshrined, even in its apparently most trivial pursuits.

One result of this was the emergence of the anecdotal scene that 'tells a story' by inviting the viewer to interpret clues, read characters and construct a sequence of events beyond the picture frame. Meaning could, however, be encoded far more subtly than by implied narrative, through selection of motifs, art-historical reference and style. In a wider overview of the period it can also be deduced by absence; paintings of people at work are far scarcer than those depicting people at play. By and large the Victorians did not decorate their walls with the imagery of the office, the factory or the scullery. (Ford Madox Brown's *Work* is, of course, a magnificent exception to this generalisation and was consciously painted as such). An artist committed to the cause of social realism might depict the plight of the overworked sempstress or stone-breaker, but such art was considered (as it was meant to be) controversial rather than comfortable. Popular paintings of the workaday round usually concentrate on such rustic activities as haymaking or fishing off an attractive stretch of coast, picturesque pursuits sufficiently distanced so as not to challenge an urban audience. Even when in 1874 Eyre Crowe exhibited a ground-breaking scene of Wigan factory girls (illustrated below) he notably chose to show them during their dinner-break rather than at their machines, and even then his work was criticised for using subject-matter unsuited to art.

The Dinner Hour, Wigan
Eyre Crowe, 1874
Manchester City Art Galleries

above:
Behind the Bar
John Henry Henshall, 1882
Museum of London, London

right:
The Awakening Conscience
William Holman Hunt, 1853-4
Tate Gallery, London

far right:
The Fair Toxophilites (cat. no.43)
William Powell Frith
Royal Albert Memorial Museum, Exeter

10 The Pursuit of Leisure

So if not work, then leisure becomes the preferred site of self-representation for the Victorians. We should be familiar with this – our own late twentieth-century culture is saturated with imagery of how we might, do or aspire to spend our spare time and how we define ourselves in the process. The most perfunctory survey of Victorian art illuminates the generation of this same syndrome: as soon as one starts looking for the leisure picture one sees it everywhere. Victoria and Albert have themselves portrayed *en route* to a fancy dress ball or enjoying a domestic moment of 'quality time'; Frith creates a sensation with a panoramic view of *Derby Day* showing the crowd rather than the race; formal portraits depict their sitters engaging in their favourite hobbies; in endless unambitious little scenes the figures add human interest by riding, dancing, reading, picnicking and playing any number of games, both organised and *ad hoc*. Even so heavyweight a piece of Pre-Raphaelite moralising as Holman Hunt's *The Awakening Conscience* (illustrated on p.10) is a leisure scene wherein a cad and his kept woman enliven their love-nest with a shared song at the piano. Obviously the concept of 'spare time' had become precious to the Victorians, a matter of pride that they lived in a society sufficiently prosperous and well-organised to permit its individual members opportunities for relaxation and the sort of diverting social interaction which could only flourish outside a pattern of unremitting labour. Most of the pastimes depicted could be viewed in a positive or even useful light: reading developed the intellect and imagination; conversation and games strengthened family bonds; days out were restorative; physical exercise promoted health; even the tending of pets was considered conducive to domestic gentleness and responsibility.

Leisure as a site of anxiety, however, could not be avoided. Crowd scenes set in public places usually include a low-life presence, reminding the viewer that the promiscuous mixture of types and classes inevitable in such a context could be dangerous to those not fortified by a clear-cut sense of their own status and propriety. Even a glittering atmosphere of wealth and fashion might signal entertainment of the wrong kind. In Alfred Elmore's *On the Brink* (illustrated left) for example, a well-dressed woman, seduced by the transient pleasures of a gambling salon, risks seduction of a far worse kind: too much unchaperoned excitement is clearly demonstrated as a dangerous pursuit. A more subtly problematic area is the relaxation of the working classes, especially in an urban setting. Country folk can be seen enjoying their simple sports, home comforts and quaint traditions at a safe distance, but their city counterparts rarely merit such unambiguous representation. Too mundane, too close to home, perhaps presumed too poor or busy to engage in any suitably picture-worthy activity, they are usually shown only to add local colour to a crowd scene or to point up a particular situation (e.g. a day trip to Brighton in a third class carriage). A caricatural element of humour in their representation can safely separate them from their audience, as can the indication that, left to their own devices, their leisure tends towards the dreary or vicious – Victorian pub scenes are by no means as convivial as their seventeenth-century counterparts (illustrated on p.10). Only towards the end of the century can an artist as 'continental' as Sickert use art to suggest the electric excitement of a cheap seat in the Gallery, where rough clothes and rowdy enthusiasm are observed as unremarkable, appropriate to their context and needful of no humorous or moralising gloss (cat. no.34).

On the Brink
Alfred Elmore, 1865
Fitzwilliam Museum, Cambridge

Leisure is uncontroversial where it functions to reinforce the accepted values of a dominant ideology. Families gather together cheerfully, children demonstrate a capacity for the innocent enjoyment of the moment, the seaside or countryside induces refreshing relaxation. As is the case throughout Victorian art, women are shown more frequently than men, often with the implication that their pursuit and display of fashionable good looks constitutes in itself an absorbing pastime suitable to their gender. An edge of modernity in their representation certainly provided a piquance for contemporary audiences. Tissot's flamboyantly stylish young women could seem dangerously 'advanced' in their little escapades (cat. no.12) and one wonders whether Lavery's solitary lady on her tricycle (cat. no.49), for example, would have seemed as uncontentious as Frith's primly earnest toxophilites (cat. no.43, illustrated on p.11).

Striving after an iconographic novelty that would reflect the ever-changing tastes of its audience helped to effect certain stylistic and generic developments in Victorian painting. Some leisure pictures explore their themes within the established formats of portraiture or populated landscape, but others have to re-assess academic traditions of composition, detail, focus and lighting in the cause of achieving a naturalistic grouping and explication of unfamiliar subject matter. A late example such as *Boulter's Lock, Sunday Afternoon*, 1895 (illustrated below left), with its bustle of activity intensifying towards the back of the scene, its abrupt truncations and air of general confusion, suggests both photographic imagery and Impressionist art as influential factors in the growing freedom of compositional organisation.

This catalogue, inevitably reflecting the limitations of what was available for loan to the exhibition it accompanies, cannot pretend to offer more than an introduction to the possibilities of its theme. It includes deliberately few images of organised sporting prowess, since these engage with pictorial traditions of heroic achievement which would merit a separate study. A decision was also made to exclude hunting scenes, a separate sub-genre with its roots in equestrian portraits and animal painting. What is at least indicated is the abundance and diversity of Victorian diversions and the ways in which recreation became an arena for representation, with contemporary modes of amusement not merely enjoyed artlessly but observed, pictorially formulated and reflected back at an audience of admiring participants.

Boulter's Lock, Sunday Afternoon
Edward John Gregory, 1895
Lady Lever Art Gallery, Port Sunlight

BY THE SEA

far left (above):
1. Ramsgate Sands, 1905
William Powell Frith

far left:
2. At the Seaside, 1886
E Aubrey Hunt

above:
3. Returning Health
Thomas Falcon Marshall

right:
4. Ramsgate Sands
Arthur Boyd Houghton

1   Ramsgate Sands (1905)   (ill. p.14)
William Powell Frith (1819-1909)
Oil on canvas, 76.2 x 154.9 cm
Signed *WP Frith 1905* (lower left)

This is an autograph copy of Frith's extremely popular painting originally shown at the R.A. in 1854 and purchased by Queen Victoria. Taking him two years to paint, the first version represented the artist's turning away from historical subjects to deal with scenes of modern life. When initially shown it was this very modernity which caught the public imagination, with Frith's photographic eye for detail capturing a scene in which the viewers might recognise themselves.

Frith visited Ramsgate (one of the more genteel seaside resorts) in 1851, making many studies of life on the beach and its rather stately architectural background, but the key to his success surely lies in his lively characterisation of a wide range of recognisable social types. From a small child trepidatiously paddling, to the elderly lady protected by her parasol, we are invited to identify characters as one might do in a novel. There is an emphasis on family groups and relationships and a general air of respectability challenged only by the boisterous band of minstrels in the middle ground to the left. They are marginalised, however, and the sweeping arc of the compostition keeps the eye of the viewer focussed on a sequence of implied narratives, permitting endless speculation about the stern, stout lady surrounded by small children, the graceful group of fashionably clad young women and the caddish young gentleman lounging beside his deeply-shaded female companion.

Russell-Cotes Art Gallery and Museum

2   At the Seaside (1886)   (ill. p.14)
E Aubrey Hunt (1855-1922)
Oil on canvas, 101 x 130 cm
Signed on a separate piece of canvas
Painting cut down

Despite a superficial similarity to Frith's *Ramsgate Sands*, (cat. no.1) the mood of this painting is considerably more relaxed and the treatment far less anecdotal. Victorian literalism has given way to a more continental feel for atmosphere above detail which might suggest the influence of the beach scenes of Boudin and an awareness of Impressionist art. Modes have clearly changed and instead of self-aware respectability in holiday guise, Hunt can present a scene of fashionable insouciance and activity. No-one seems the least concerned by the bathers, male and female, whose costumes show that the sea itself and not just the beach has, by the 1880s, become an arena for leisure.

Government Art Collection

3 Returning Health (c.1860s) (ill. p.15)
Thomas Falcon Marshall (1818-78)
Oil on canvas, 46.8 x 71 cm
Nottingham only

Rather than describing a bustling resort scene, the Liverpool genre painter Marshall interprets the seaside as the sort of quiet, unspoiled spot where an invalid might go to convalesce in the health-giving ocean air. The pallid girl in the centre, accompanied perhaps by mother and sister, looks wistfully at the sturdy, fresh-faced local children. Despite their bare feet, rough clothes and the suggestion that they are already working for their living along the seashore, the fisher children here represent an idealised notion of the good, simple, outdoor life. By contrast the well-dressed young lady is a delicate flower who needs careful nurturing. In a slightly different alternative version of the painting, Marshall replaced the children with a boy and an elderly (but hale) fisherman carrying nets, while further fishing activity visible on the distant shoreline reinforced the notion of active work as part of a robust 'natural' life enjoyed by peasants but denied to the gently bred. This concept reverses the more predictable viewpoint by presenting 'leisure' as fraught with poignancy when set beside the advantages of open-air occupation.

Worthing Museum and Art Gallery

4 Ramsgate Sands (c.1863) (ill. p.15)
Arthur Boyd Houghton (1836-75)
Oil on canvas, 24.1 x 29.8 cm
Signed with initials

A well-travelled artist with a reputation for genial bonhomie and bohemianism, Houghton's short life was nonetheless coloured by misfortune – he lost the sight of one eye in a childhood accident, his adored wife Susan died after only three years of marriage and his own early death from cirrhosis was a result of steady drinking. His artistic career presents a similar dichotomy in that he was amongst the greatest of Victorian graphic artists, illustrating numerous books and magazines, but harboured an ambition to produce the sort of serious history paintings which would be classed as High Art. Somewhere between the two extremes, during the 1860s, he produced a series of fresh, lively and intensely personal little paintings, usually showing members of his family, which depicted cheerful relaxation either at home or on some suitable excursion. These small, informal works do not always have fixed titles. *Ramsgate Sands* has also been known as *Out of Doors*, and whilst the former title allies it to Frith's unavoidable prototype and to an earlier Ramsgate scene by Houghton himself (1860-61, in the collection of the Johannesburg Art Gallery), the latter stresses its sense of visual immediacy. This reinforces the notion that it was at least begun on the spot, with the East Cliff in the background. The central figure, painfully over-wrapped to modern eyes and quite absorbed in her book, is Susan Houghton, towards whom her two-year-old son, Arthur, toddles. The most surprising touch, however, is the pair of peeping heads (most probably Grace Houghton and the painter, Tourrier) gazing out at the viewer and, by implication, at the artist, from behind Susan's voluminous skirts. Their deliberately capricious position and her complete unawareness of their presence only make sense as a family joke, the equivalent of someone popping up behind the subject just as a photograph is being taken.

Tate Gallery. Presented by Miss Helen Devitt in memory of Sit William Devitt Bt. 1924

above:
5. Yarmouth Jetty, Evening
Sidney Felix Howitt

right:
6. Yarmouth Beach
attributed to **Anthony Sandys**

above:
8. The Bathers
William McTaggart

5   Yarmouth Jetty, Evening, 1890   (ill. p.18)
Sidney Felix Howitt (1845-1915)
Pencil and watercolour on paper, 20.6 x 27.4 cm
Signed in monogram *S.F.H. 1890* (bottom right)

This little picture combines the watercolour tradition of land- or sea-scapes painted to evoke a specific sense of place with the iconography of the leisure picture. Yarmouth Jetty and its spatial relationship with both the sea and the promenade provides the defining motif of the composition, but the character of Victorian Yarmouth, a fishing port which had by this time become a family resort, can only be expressed by the inclusion of figures. This is a relaxed scene, in which a stroll along the beach or the promise of a bracing carriage ride are shown as the activities appropriate to a seaside holiday.

Norfolk Museums Service (Norwich Castle Museum)

6   Looking for the Mail Packet (1861)   (ill. p.22)
Henry Garland (1834-1913)
Oil on canvas, 52 x 47 cm
Inscribed *H Garland 1861* (lower left)

Garland's fresh, lively painting offers an instructive compendium of Victorian leisure motifs. A well-dressed family has strolled along the seaside cliff top in order to provide Papa with the pleasure of spotting the incoming mail packet through his suitably nautical telescope. His straw hat and the very lightweight, loose-sleeved blouse worn by his daughter indicate sunny weather, though both women sport Paisley shawls. The outing also manages to incorporate taking the small lap-dog for a walk and permitting the exercise of ladylike accomplishments, for the young woman has been sketching the sea-scape in watercolours. This descriptive depiction of shared family pleasures, however, actually provides the setting for a humorous-sentimental little narrative which indicates courtship as yet another activity suitable for a relaxed summer day. While her father's attention is distracted, the girl makes contact with an alternative 'mail packet', receiving a letter from (or perhaps sending one to) a gentleman admirer seen in the distance, *via* his large, well-trained dog, whose presence attracts the attention of the be-ribboned spaniel.

York City Art Gallery (bequeathed by John Burton, 1882)

7   Yarmouth Beach (1860-65)   (ill. p.18)
attributed to Anthony Sandys (1806-83)
Oil on canvas, 36 x 46 cm

At one stage this painting was attributed to Frederick Sandys, an artist associated with the later pre-Raphaelites, and in common with his work it does utilise the portrait format for what is actually a 'fancy head' of an unidentified female sitter, placing her against an almost unconnected background and fetishistically describing the texture of her hair, costume and accessories. The figure's loose hair, shaded eyes and air of mannered absorption add a note of perverse self-awareness to the display of her charms, which would also be in keeping with the style of Frederick. The handling, however, is visibly coarser than this artist's mature style and the prissiness of the feathered hat, stitched gloves and tiny parasol seems far from his exotically-robed romantic heroines.

A more plausible attribution gives the work to Anthony Sandys, Frederick's father, a textile dyer who became a drawing master and artist, exhibiting with various Norwich societies. Perhaps he was attempting a modern dress variant of his son's lush female 'fancy heads'. The wide sky and seascape (identifiable by its Nelson monument at Yarmouth Harbour) has an airiness and naturalism at odds with the stylised treatment of the figure and points to Anthony's earlier connection with the Norwich School of landscape. It is the background, with its suggestion of a seaside holiday, which adds an extra resonance to the scene – the coast is painted not so much as a visually realistic setting but as an additional accessory to the image, a backdrop to the still-life of pretty features and garments, giving a reason for the parasol and contextualising the sense of open-air leisure combined with stylish display. Details of the costume suggest a date in the early 1860s. The sitter might be Emily Sandys, daughter of Anthony and herself an artist.

Thetford Town Council

8 By the Sea
(ill. below)

George Frederick Watts (1817-1904)
Oil on canvas, 39.6 x 48.2 cm

Like Sandys' *Yarmouth Beach* (cat. no.7), this small painting merely uses a seaside setting (here indicated by the loosely painted sky and sea) as a background which will impart a holiday air to the female head placed against it. Watts' Titianesque handling makes this more of a study in the textures of feathers, hair and skin than a tight depiction of fashionable detail.

Victoria Art Gallery, Bath and North East Somerset Council

9 The Bathers (1886)
(ill. p.19)

William McTaggart (1835-1910)
Oil on canvas, 19.1 x 26.7 cm
Signed *W McTaggart 1886* (bottom left)

In common with several other Scottish artists of the late nineteenth century, McTaggart moved away from Victorian anecdotalism towards a freer approach to both subject and brushwork. Like the Impressionists he used paint and colour to create the sensations of the scene rather than to tell a story, and some of his later work was produced *en plein air*. Of his many paintings of children at play (he had fourteen of his own from two marriages) this is a particularly lively example conveying the boys' spontaneous delight at the chance of discarding their clothes and splashing into the waves.

Dundee Arts and Heritage (McManus Galleries)

BY THE SEA/ON THE WATER

above:
11. A Conversation at Sea
Allan J Hook

right:
9. Looking for the Mail Packet
Henry Garland

far right:
12. Boarding the Yacht
James (Jacques Joseph) Tissot

ON THE WATER

10 Outward Bound

Leopold Augustus Egg (1816-63)
Millboard mounted as a drawing, 17 x 23 cm

The robust pleasures of boating or sailing, which might encompass anything from a canoe on the canal to an ocean cruise, became increasingly popular as a source of exercise or excitement offering a variety of scenery to be enjoyed in the open air. The title of Egg's vibrant little study, in alliance with its daringly unconventional composition, captures some of the exhilaration of sailing away from the land and feeling free from constraint. In fact it is the female figure, enthusiastically wielding her telescope, who conveys the sense of adventure. Her male companion takes the chance to relax, shedding his hat and lying back luxuriously to smoke a cigarette. Egg himself, for reasons of health, lived on the Continent for much of his life, and would have known the bracing excitement proffered by sea air and the motion of the waves.

The Visitors of the Ashmolean Museum

11 Conversation at Sea (ill. p.22)
Allan J Hook (b.1853, *fl.* until 1896)
Oil on canvas, 74.2 x 116.8 cm
Signed *AJ Hook/1885* (lower right)

Like Egg's *Outward Bound*, this shows a ship not as a working environment for crew and captain but as the site for relaxation under invigorating circumstances. The woman is seated on deck to enjoy the air and the sight of the sea, while a gentleman in the holiday informality of shirt sleeves engages in *al fresco* conversation. Since they are actually at sea, out of sight of land, the couple could be serious travellers rather than just day-trippers sailing around the coast. The woman's practical costume provides an interesting contrast to the feminine fashions in Tissot's *Boarding the Yacht* (cat. no.12) and the binoculars she holds indicates that she is more interested in the trip than in her personal appearance.

Leeds Museums and Galleries (City Art Gallery)

12 Boarding the Yacht (c.1872-6) (ill. p.23)
James (Jacques Joseph) Tissot (1836-1902)
Oil on canvas, 71 x 53.4 cm
Nottingham only

Tissot must count as the most continental of Victorian artists. Born at Nantes, he studied and exhibited in Paris before moving to London in 1871 following the fall of the Commune. He returned to Paris in 1882, but during his eleven years in England he created his own distinctive form of the conversation piece, in which acutely elegant female figures (modelled latterly by his beloved mistress Kathleen Newton) populate a world of fashionable leisure. His depictions were sufficiently detailed to suit Victorian tastes, yet hinted in their unconventional compositional arrangements at Tissot's peripheral connection with the Impressionist movement. *Boarding the Yacht* is one of a series of works produced *c.1872-6* in which the same models, costumes and Thameside settings recur. Though never shown together, such close variations suggest a themed sequence and Tissot may have had in mind a projected series in which 'la belle anglaise' was depicted almost photographically at her typical amusements. The woman on the right is Margaret Kennedy, wife of John Freebody, captain of the *Carisbrooke Castle* which she is shown boarding. The other woman is her sister, and their bearded companion also turns up in several shipboard scenes. *The Captain and the Mate* (1873, Private Collection) for example shows the same man and both women wearing the same fashionable costumes with a slight variety of accessories. That both Tissot's parents had been involved in the fashion trade may be of relevance to

the way he used the expertly observed minutiae of costume for maximum visual impact. His detailed depiction of the ship's fittings and rigging is equally convincing and probably relates to his boyhood spent on the Loire estuary.

To regard paintings such as this as little more than 'still-lives' of fashion-plate outfits and the accoutrements of a leisured existence minimises their contemporary meaning. Victorian audiences were very alert to the implications of relationship and social status encoded in Tissot's elaborately dressed and coiffed young women, who clearly enjoy the excitements offered by modern life under circumstances where the rigid proprieties of earlier social codes were becoming relaxed. About to join a group on the upper deck, the unchaperoned women here self-confidently accept the courteous attention of the naval officer. Despite the conspicuous consumption apparent in their outfits, these figures do not belong to the upper reaches of society and might appear dangerously 'unfixed' in their suggestion of wealth and privilege allied to enjoyment and independence. Here we see the *nouveaux riches* frivolously breaking the rules. The fact that these pictures deliberately flaunt the reassuring domesticity of the late Victorian family group spending its leisure together no doubt gave them an added piquancy and modernity, though Tissot could, on occasion, misjudge this: *The Thames* (Wakefield Art Gallery), 1876, showing a young man relaxing with two ladies, was actually considered to be morally questionable and, in the words of *The Graphic*, 'More French, shall we say, than English?'

Private Collection

THE PROMENADE

13 Lewes Crescent (c.1838) (ill. p.29)
George Bryant Campion (1796-1870)
Watercolour and bodycolour on paper,
22.6 x 35.3 cm

Unlike many popular Victorian seaside towns, Brighton's history as a resort long predates the nineteenth century. Its identity as an important fishing centre was augmented by the attractions of its sea-water cure, possibly as early as the seventeenth century but certainly in booming fashion by the mid-eighteenth century. Bathing machines appear to have been in use there as early as 1754. Even before the opening of the railway in 1841, a regular coach service from London and the patronage of the Prince Regent had made it the most fashionable resort of the early nineteenth century. At this period, unless one was there purely for reasons of health, the emphasis was less on the beach than on the social life offered by the town, with its elegant Georgian architecture and opportunity to promenade in the latest fashions. Only later in the century did the beach itself become the focus for family outings and entertainment throughout the summer months, though Brighton regrouped its earlier reputation for gentility with an annual winter season of more polite, aristocratic flavour.

Campion's watercolour, which can be dated from its reproduction as an aquatint in Mason's *Illustrations of Brighton* (published in 1838), shows the resort at the very beginning of Victoria's reign, between its Regency heyday and subsequent popularisation by a wider social range of day-trippers. Lewes Crescent, which was completed by 1828, here becomes the backdrop for a promenade of well-mannered elegance, where gentlemen raise their hats to the bonnetted, veiled and parasoled ladies who enjoy the fresh air without risking their complexions to the sun. A few hearty souls have ventured onto the beach, but there is no entertainment offered beyond the gentle exercise of strolling or riding whilst observing the passing scene. For those less energetic, transport varies from the open carriages and four to the sedate pace offered by a goat cart. These latter would subsequently find their way onto the beach, where later in the reign they offered an alternative to seaside donkey rides.

Royal Pavilion, Art Gallery and Museums, Brighton and Hove

14 A Stormy Day at Brighton (1905) (ill. p.29)
Charles Conder (1868-1909)
Oil on canvas, 50.5 x 91.7 cm
Signed *Conder 1905* (bottom right)

Though born in Victorian London, Conder spent his adolescence in Australia and subsequently studied art in Paris. Connections with such artists as Toulouse-Lautrec, Whistler and Beardsley help contextualise Conder as belonging to the late-nineteenth century *avant garde*, so while his choice of the Brighton seafront as a subject for at least three paintings during 1904-5 might seem to hark back to Victorian convention, his handling of the visual material presented by the resort demonstrates a mould-breaking awareness of European trends. Eschewing the anecdotalism implied by a rainy day at the seaside, where hardy, well-wrapped holidaymakers trudge dauntlessly through the onslaught of the elements, he actually diminishes any sense of place or implied narrative in favour of an exciting handling of paint, where visible brush-strokes function undisguisedly to convey the sense of wind, rain and sea. This could act as a coda to the Victorian seaside leisure picture in more ways than one – Conder's own visits to Brighton in 1904 and 1906 notably failed to restore the ailing health that was a legacy of intemperate artistic bohemianism and the painter died in 1909.

Royal Pavilion, Art Gallery and Museums, Brighton and Hove

15 The Avenue, Wildernesse (c.1876-86) (ill. p.7)
Valentine Cameron Prinsep (1838-1904)
Oil on canvas, 95.5 x 76.2 cm

The promenade here is a little leisurely exercise taken by an extended family group and their guests in the congenial surroundings of their country house grounds. Wildernesse, at Sevenoaks, Kent was a seat of Lord Hillingdon and some of the figures can be identified as portraits. It seems likely that this relaxed, informal painting captures the atmosphere of an actual gathering at which the artist was present as a guest. Not only Prinsep but also Poynter, Dickie Doyle and Watts were artistic friends of the Hillingdon family. The women in the foreground are daughters of the 3rd Earl of Harewood: the one in white is Lady Louisa Mills (afterwards Lady Hillingdon), on the right is the Countess of Wharncliffe and standing is Lady George Hamilton.

Birmingham Museums and Art Gallery

16 Old Men in Rockingham Park
William Bouner Gash (1870-1928)

Oil on canvas, 87 x 100.5 cm
Signed (bottom right corner)
Exeter only

Aside from the occasional 'Social Realist' scene of the workhouse, representations of the elderly in Victorian genre painting almost invariably place their figures in a familial context. Darby and Joan domesticity or affectionate relationships between grandparents and their grandchildren are favourite ways of contextualising old age within safe social patterns. The Kettering artist, WB Gash, in common with other painters working across the turn of the century, abandons reassuring sentimentality in favour of an un-idealised, freely handled rethinking of his theme. Here the old men are grouped together in the enforced leisure of age and infirmity, where movement is slow and repose appreciated. The mood, however, is still that of a social gathering, with a sense of shared time, comradeship and quiet enjoyment conveyed by gesture, expression and the interaction of figures and landscape.

Alfred East Art Gallery, Kettering

17 Punch and Judy (c.1860)
Arthur Boyd Houghton (1836-75)
Oil on canvas, 35.5 x 25.5 cm
Signed with monogram

In several paintings from the 1860s, Houghton took the idea of a panoramic microcosm of London life in the mode of Frith or Hicks and scaled it down to suit a small, crowded canvas. In this example the apparent piling up of the figures and the deceptively casual choice of a viewpoint that conceals the face of the boy carrying the basket, and shows the puppeteer's booth only from the side, heightens a sense of almost snapshot immediacy. Though other pictures from this period show the bustle of street life, the recruitment of soldiers and the plight of poor itinerant singers, here the subject is an oasis of urban entertainment where the focus of attention for adults and infants alike is a Punch and Judy show sufficiently amusing even to attract the passing gaze of the conspicuously tall, bewhiskered soldier who towers above the women and children.

Tate Gallery. Purchased 1922

above:
17. Punch and Judy
Arthur Boyd Houghton

far right (above):
14. A Stormy Day at Brighton
Charles Conder

far right:
13. Lewes Crescent
George Bryant Campion

OUTDOOR ACTIVITIES

18 Stoolball at Tarring (1856)

Edward Martin (fl.1845-61)

Watercolour heightened with bodycolour on paper,
37 x 72 cm
Signed (bottom right)

Stoolball is a game similar to cricket but played with a round-headed bat and employing milking stools as wickets and belongs almost exclusively to Sussex. A local peculiarity is the acceptable and enthusiastic involvement of women as players. With no professional status the game remained essentially one for small communities and this watercolour is as much a portrait of the place where it was played (still identifiable as Tarring) as it is an account of the game itself.

Worthing Museum and Art Gallery

19 Shuttlecock

Alexander Hohenlohe Burr (1835-99)

Oil on canvas, 49.5 x 73.7 cm
Signed *A Burr* (lower left)

Burr was a popular Scottish painter (many of his works were engraved) of history and genre scenes. In pictures such as *Blind Man's Buff* and *Grandad's Delight* he displayed a fondness for depicting children in reassuringly uncomplicated situations of family leisure and affection. Here a scene of rustic simplicity centres on an elderly man playing shuttlecock at amusingly close quarters with a young child (the short hair suggests this to be a boy, though still young enough to be dressed in an infant's frock). Their sport attracts the attention of two girls who neglect their doll to watch, aiding the obvious implication that this is a happy family group – mother in the cottage, father and an older son coming back from shooting and grandfather amusing the sisters and younger brother.

Battledore and shuttlecock (referring to the wooden bats and feathered projectile) is a simple game which seems to have been played in Britain since at least the fourteenth century. Around 1870 it was developed into the competitive form of badminton, but Victorian artists remained more attracted to depicting the older game as a typical mode of healthy exercise and amusement for children and young ladies in almost any period or setting (see cat. no.46).

Glasgow Museum; Art Gallery and Museum, Kelvingrove

right:
19. Shuttlecock
Alexander Hohenlohe Burr

above:
22. A Scottish Fair
John Phillip

right:
23. A Border Fair
John Ritchie

20 The Curlers (c.1835) (ill. p.31)
Sir George Harvey (1806-76)
Oil on canvas, 35.9 x 79.4 cm
Signed (lower left)

In a flourishing national school of genre painting, Scottish artists produced many scenes of what might be termed indigenous leisure pursuits, where such activities as shooting, skating, bowls and golf were depicted with a distinct flavour of the country, its landscape and its people. There is a gentle humour in the treatment here of a curling match where the local minister, watched by the laird, has just thrown the penultimate stone while the final one can be seen waiting behind the two men. Its passage across the ice, facilitated by the 'sooping up' of the surface, becomes a focus for avid attention and excitement, as its ultimate position amongst the other stones may decide the victor. This is obviously a village game, where everyone knows each other, and a sense of community enthusiasm for the sport of the season is laced with a touch of local rivalry. The frozen loch and misty grey sky convey a strong sense of the chill northern winter which in no way subdues the energy of the Scottish sportsmen.

National Gallery of Scotland, Edinburgh

21 The Shooting Match (ill. p.31)
John Faed (1820-1902)
Oil on canvas, 45 x 76 cm
Signed *John Faed RSA* (bottom right)

Faed specialised in scenes of Highland genre and here produces a picture which is as much about a particular land- and sky-scape as it is a study of idiosyncratic character types engaging in outdoor competition. To the left the competitors register and in the centre of the composition a standing group prepares its guns, but the actual shooting is pictorially unspectacular: lying on a rough blanket the marksman fires at an airborne target, presumably some kind of clay pigeon. Faed's interest is less on the sport than on the sense of a social occasion in the countryside and the response of the spectators. From the left two well-dressed ladies approach the event, on the right a countrywoman shields her frightened child from the noise and behind the *ad hoc* desk is a bustle of figures talking, eating and drinking.

Sefton MBC Leisure Services Dept, Arts and Cultural Services Section, The Atkinson Art Gallery, Southport

22 A Scottish Fair (1851)
John Phillip (1817-67)
Oil on canvas, 88.9 x 134.6 cm

A northern European tradition of representing country fairs might be traced back to the work of Breughel and, even at its roots, raises issues of iconographic intention. Such fairs were real, valuable events, but images of them rarely document actual occasions. Instead they group together collections of picturesque characters, stalls and activities to produce a generalised notion of a rural gathering that combines leisure, trade and socialising. The end result always emphasises enough of the rustic messiness of the proceedings to ensure its appeal to urban patrons.

Phillip's fair was produced during his years as a painter of Scottish genre in the mode of Wilkie. The style of the figures seems rather dated for 1851, especially the incongruously pale and elegant peasant girl in the foreground. Trade in livestock is obviously as important here as is idle amusement and the picture plays up the notion of Scotland as an area immune from the vagaries of fashionable life where country traditions were unthinkingly preserved.

Towneley Hall Art Gallery and Museums, Burnley Borough Council

23 A Border Fair
John Ritchie (*fl.*1858-75)
Oil on canvas, 69 x 106.5 cm
Signed in monogram (bottom right)

By contrast with the Phillip, Ritchie's canvas shows the influence of Frith's panoramic scenes of modern life in the anecdotalism with which its bustling crowd is portrayed. His *Border Fair* is less distinctly rustic than Phillip's Scottish one; not only the town in the background but also the clothes of the crowd (some of which have pretensions to fashion) suggest an urban/rural borderland which accords well with the commerce/leisure character of the occasion. A busy sheepdog in the upper left corner provides a reminder that to a farming community the trade in livestock constituted a vital element of such events. In the foreground, however, there is more emphasis on the amusements of buying family goods, toys or comestibles, having one's fortune told, getting into a fight or enjoying the novelty of the scene. Across the background stretches a gaudily painted booth which seems to offer both costumed drama and sideshow curiosities to the paying customer, introducing a note of tawdry fairground glamour.

Laing Art Gallery, Newcastle upon Tyne (Tyne and Wear Museums)

AT THE CREASE

above:
24. Cricket Match at Edenside
Sam Bough

far right (above):
25. A Country Cricket Match
John Robertson Reid

far right:
26. The Winner of the Match
Henry Garland

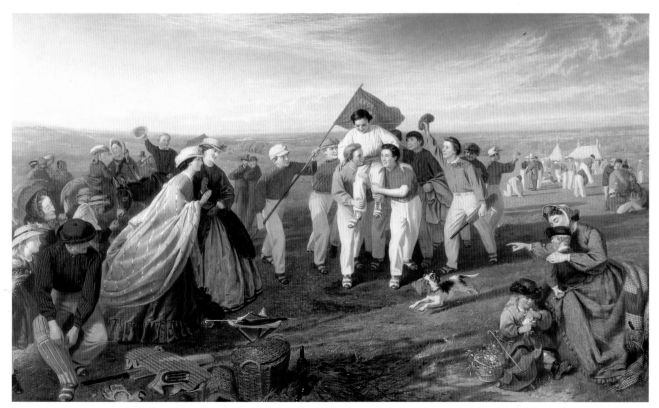

AT THE CREASE

24 Cricket Match at Edenside (c.1844) (ill. p.34)
Sam Bough (1822-78)
Oil on canvas, 65.3 x 92.2 cm

Although he described it as 'a shabby place that cannot afford an exhibition' Bough's training and early career in Carlisle, the city of his birth, inspired some of his most distinctive images. Too easily categorised as Romantic landscapes, these scenes are often full of idiosyncratic details which demonstrate the artist's awareness of the ways in which human occupation and activity added their own character to the countryside. This fine example probably commemorates a real event and was possibly painted for Mr Howe, one of the umpires shown in the painting. A calm and idyllic scene to modern eyes, the distant skyline actually includes chimneys, factory buildings and ships' masts on Carlisle canal. The Edenside cricket ground to the north of the city was the site of matches between the Carlisle and Northumberland clubs and in its own way the wide expanse of neatly mown green also represents an observation on landscape manipulated to social needs.

In its format and especially its emphasis on a wide atmospheric sky-scape, the painting remains a landscape within which cricket happens to be the controlling activity. Despite the small scale of the figures, however, Bough manages to present a lively view of an occasion as convivial as it is competitive. A foreground group of fashionably dressed spectators watches the action with casual interest. At the other side of the field, however, a considerable crowd is massed, many of them protected by open-sided tents. A contemporary account of a similar match played at the same ground on 8 June 1844 refers to a large party dining together in one of the tents and mentions that 'the excellent brass band of the 43rd regiment was on the ground and added much to the gaiety of the day'. The scarlet tunics of the military band add a small but significant note of colour and Bough makes an equally effective use of the whites of the players dotted across the ground. The umpires wear formal top hats.

Tullie House Museum and Art Gallery, Carlisle

25 A Country Cricket Match (1878) (ill. p.35)
John Robertson Reid (1851-1926)
Oil on canvas, 106.7 x 181.6 cm
Inscribed: *John R Reid 78* (bottom left)

Like Garland's picture (cat. no.26), this is at least as much a depiction of spectators, surroundings and a still-life of cricketing equipment as it is a representation of the game itself, and it, too, conveys the holiday atmosphere of an informal occasion. The style, however, is quite different from Garland's mid-Victorian brightness. Reid was involved with the Scottish Impressionists and was also influenced by such Social Realists as Bastien Lepage and although his mood is much gentler than theirs, this picture does convey the sense of an unposed scene caught at the edge of the action.

The group of village elders and lounging lads, several of them still wearing the traditional country smocks, who watch in a desultory manner from the refreshment table, would suggest a game of purely local interest being played on the rustic green. Several other figures, however, are more fashionably dressed and the various hearty young men in decoratively coloured caps indicate that the village team has actually been pitted against opponents of a quite different class, perhaps members of a house party from the local manor. The foremost of these, a caddishly charming young blade, has abandoned interest in the game in favour of flirting with the pretty country waitress. The glimpse of the match at the top right not only shows a batsman taking strike but also includes (as does Bough's *Cricket Match at Edenside* [cat. no.24]) an umpire who holds a bat. It had been usual practice for the bat to be touched in order to register that a run had been scored and although this was an outmoded rule by the 1870s, Reid clearly indicates that it survived in country matches.

Tate Gallery. Presented by Sir Henry Tate, 1894

26 The Winner of the Match, Excelsior Cricket Club (1864)

(ill. p.35)

Henry Garland (fl.1854-90)
Oil on canvas, 78.7 x 134.5 cm
Signed and dated 1864

This effervescent genre painting avoids the compositional difficulties presented by a small number of players spread across a large ground by representing not the match itself but its celebratory aftermath. The game has been played and the smiling lad who brought his team to victory is carried shoulder-high by his delighted comrades. To judge from their ages this was a junior, or school, team – the Excelsior Club is probably an invention of the artist. Their audience would seem to consist mainly of fond relatives and friends – perhaps the lady in the elegant grey mantle is a proud mama. Only the little girl making a posy of flowers seems unmoved, as small sisters so often are. The young players have not adopted uniform whites and their coloured shirts add much to the lighthearted mood of the picture, as does the enthusiastic involvement of the family dog. The speculative gaze of the two older men in the background suggests that they are talent-spotting and that this young man's future in the game is secured.

MCC Museum

27 Gentlemen v Players at Lords in the Pavilion Enclosure, 1891

(ill. below)

Sir Robert Ponsonby Staples (1853-1943)
Black and grey wash with heightened white,
35.5 x 71 cms
Monogrammed (lower right)

This annual occasion had become part of the sporting social calendar for the *haute monde* and attracted a crowd of fashionably-dressed enthusiasts to Lords to see the match and to be seen. As was usual, some observers watch from the comfortable and lofty vantage point of their own carriage – in this instance the Earl of Londesborough's coach can be identified. Also recognisable to a contemporary audience are several of the players waiting in the enclosure before the Pavilion Building. These include V E Walker, President of the MCC, and the heavily bearded W G Grace. The reason that so many likenesses are emphasised here is because this picture functioned as a study for a magazine illustration in *Black and White* (4 July 1891) which was, in effect, a group portrait of those involved in a specific occasion. In fact the match recorded did not, in 1891, take place until 6-8 July, when, owing to rain, it was drawn.

MCC Museum

A DAY OUT

28   To Brighton and Back for 3s 6d (1859)
Charles Rossiter (b.1827, *fl*.1852-90)
Oil on canvas, 61 x 76 cm
Signed *C Rossiter* (bottom right)

Rossiter's painting appears to be unique in depicting the less than luxurious conditions of third-class excursion travel on the railway. The first third-class excursion fare was advertised in 1849, with the obvious intention of attracting a class of passenger for whom considerations of economy ranked higher than those of comfort. The third-class carriage did boast a roof, but its sides were open to the elements. Quite aside from the promiscuous mix of tightly-packed fellow passengers, the hardy traveller was at the mercy of the weather to an alarming degree, as described in the Railway Monitor:

"Make up your mind for unmitigated hail, rain, sleet, snow, thunder and lightening. Look out for a double allowance of smoke, dust, dirt and everything that is disagreeable". (Quoted in Brian Haresnape, *Design for Steam*, London, 1968, p.17).

The fact that Rossiter includes the fare of 3s 6d (17.5p) as part of the title makes it sound like a contemporary joke – presumably this had become a catchphrase for a cheap day out from London. Even third-class travel, however, would not have been within reach of the very poor, nor would they necessarily have had enough time on their hands for a day at the seaside. Rossiter's picture is not about the limited leisure of the indigenous, but an amusing description of diversion on a budget, the joke being that the conditions of travel are so far from luxurious. The men depicted have a rather threadbare look and the centre of the composition is filled with the bustle of women and children packed together rather too closely for comfort. The older woman on the front seat is perhaps a governess and the standing girl may be a nursemaid, taking their small charges for a day in the sea air. The young couple, effectively in a world of their own within which the crush all around them goes unnoticed, could be courting, but Rossiter gives them no air of frivolity to suggest flirtation or philandering. It seems more likely that they are a young married couple, and as the newspaper in the woman's lap is called *The Family Herald* the implication may be that she is pregnant and visiting the coast for its healthful air. Her pensive gaze and the man's solicitous proximity would tend to reinforce this interpretation. As usual in mid-Victorian paintings about the seaside, everyone seems heavily wrapped up and equipped with shawls, hats, scarves and parasols. The large umbrella pushed through the carriage opening to the left is there, however, less against the weather than to provide some protection from the soot, smut and grit that were prevailing annoyances in open-sided vehicles.

Birmingham Museums and Art Gallery

AT THE RACES

29 Epsom Downs, 1863 (1871)
Aaron Green after Alfred Hunt
Oil on canvas, 84 x 120 cm
Inscribed *A. Green 1871* (lower right)
Nottingham only

One of the most popular Victorian pictures of contemporary life was WP Frith's *Derby Day* (R.A. 1858) with which he consolidated the success of *Ramsgate Sands* (cat. no.1). Frith's painting was by no means the first representation of the Derby, which had been instituted as an annual event on Epsom Downs in 1780, but his panoramic survey of the holiday atmosphere prevailing amongst a crowd of spectators helped set a fashion for images in which the audience itself constituted the subject.

Artists who emulated his success included Alfred Hunt, whose 1863 painting, *At Epsom Downs*, was engraved as a popular print soon after its completion and copied in

1871 by Aaron Green. It follows Frith in positioning the grandstand and racecourse towards the back of the canvas and concentrates instead on the bustling activity of the crowd. These are not necessarily dedicated followers of the turf, but people on a day out, and the social mixture is essential to the mood of the picture. Red-coated soldiers and city swells (some of the gentlemen sporting the distinctive puggarees, or coloured veils wound around their top hats, which could be used to protect the face from dust) rub shoulders with beggars, mountebanks and acrobats. In the foregound a shabby pedlar is selling the little wooden dolls and pasteboard noses which had become traditional Derby Day merchandise. Assorted skittle games in the centre of the compostition seem to have entirely distracted their players from the race, while to the right, in a motif which is an obvious variation on Frith, the prosperous enjoy a picnic as the hungry look on.

City Museum and Art Gallery, Stoke on Trent

30 The Race Meeting (1853)
Sir John Everett Millais (1829-96)
Pen and black ink with brown ink on paper,
24.9 x 17.7 cm
Inscribed with initials and dated

This drawing was directly inspired by a visit to Epsom in 1853, when the artist's Pre-Raphaelite affiliations were still attracting him towards realistic images of the problems of contemporary life. Based on an incident he had observed, he shows the darker side of a holiday event which inevitably tempted gamblers to dip too deep. The race is over, a luxurious picnic eaten and a fashionably dressed young woman sobs as her male companion indicates with an insouciant gesture, echoed by the Derby doll in his hat, that his money has gone. With the originality that characterised his early years, Millais has here pre-dated one of the themes of Frith's *Derby Day* by several years.

The Visitors of the Ashmolean Museum

31 Before the Race, Nottingham (1865)
John Holland Snr (1829-86)
Oil on canvas, 43.8 x 68.6 cm
Signed *J. Holland 1865* (on foreground basket)

Nottingham artist John Holland Snr not only produced a local variation on Frith's *Derby Day* but expanded the idea by pairing *Before the Race* with *After the Race* (also shown in 1865, current whereabouts unknown). The latter includes the collapse of a viewing stand in the pandemonium subsequent to the race, but even in the former the mood is more riotous and less respectable than most paintings on similar themes. More than one fight seems to be breaking out and a large Aunt Sally stall further suggests a mood of aggression. There is also the inevitable foreground group of picnickers, but the artist stands sufficiently far back from his subject to be able to concentrate on the distinctive lie of the land at Nottingham racecourse rather than the minute details of the spectators invading it.

City of Nottingham Museums; Castle Museum and Art Gallery

THEATRICAL ENTERTAINMENTS

32 Queen Victoria at the Opera (1838)
Edmund Thomas Parry
Oil on canvas, 31.8 x 48.3 cm

Although this is ostensibly a portrait of the young monarch, she has been idealised to a vision of *Keepsake* prettiness which diminishes individuality in favour of a conventionalised femininity. A gently smiling figurehead at the front of the Royal Box, she is obviously on public display, although Victoria's genuine enthusiasm for musical and theatrical entertainments simultaneously makes this an image of regal leisure. Her expensive, frivolously fashionable attire suggests the same dichotomy – that a delight in her clothes and jewels represented a personal pleasure for the Queen whilst also constituting an element in her glittering offical image.

The FORBES Magazine Collection

33 At the Opera (1855)
William Powell Frith (1819-1909)
Oil on canvas, 34.9 x 45 cm (detail)

Unlike Parry's *Queen Victoria at the Opera* (cat. no.32), which it superficially resembles, this is not a portrait. The figure is a generalised type of fashionable beauty suitably attired in evening dress, silk gloves and opera cloak. Although her gaze is presumably directed at the stage and she carries opera glasses, the subject is little more than an excuse for a 'fancy picture' where a motif from a contemporary leisured existence provides the setting for an attractive figure.

Harris Museum and Art Gallery, Preston

34 Noctes Ambrosianae (1906)
Walter Richard Sickert (1860-1942)
Oil on canvas, 63.5 x 76.2 cm
Signed *Sickert* (bottom right)

Sickert was one of the most cosmopolitan of late-nineteenth century artists working in Britain, to the extent he hardly seems to merit the term 'Victorian' at all. His connections with Degas and the Impressionists, with Whistler, and with Steer and the New English Art Club fed into a development of both style and imagery which not only challenged an already fading anecdotalism but also presented a lively alternative.

His first music-hall pictures, shown towards the end of the 1880s, immediately earned such a severe critical response as to make it apparent that the artist had located a troublesome area in the 'respectable' consciousness by depicting the kind of entertainment considered cheap, vulgar and morally dangerous. Sickert took no moralising stance, attempting instead to convey the sense of place and occasion, the warmth and energy and the thrilling darkness of these unpretendingly popular venues. Both audience and performers can be the focus of his work, but in this example dating from his renewed interest in the theme during 1906 it is the rowdy lads in the gallery, with their eager physical stances and eerily-lit faces, who convey the message of working class leisure taken with gusto at a public entertainment. The setting is quite specifically the gallery of the Middlesex Music Hall in Drury Lane, this being one of four views all painted by Sickert on canvasses of the same size.

City of Nottingham Museums; Castle Museum and Art Gallery

THE ENJOYMENT OF ART

35 Public Opinion (c.1863)
George B O'Neill (1828-1917)
Oil on canvas, 53.3 x 78.7 cm
Signed *G.B. O'Neill* (bottom right)
Nottingham only

The notions that looking at art provided edification as well as entertainment and that the promotion and development of public taste represented a vaguely defined but undisputable good, fuelled a growing emphasis on 'art for all' during Victoria's reign. Certainly the expansion of a leisured middle class with sufficient time and interest did build up a wider audience for galleries, and the Royal Academy's massive Summer Exhibition came to represent a popular annual event for anyone remotely interested in contemporary art. (Attendance reached a peak in 1879, when the show drew 391,197 visitors). An entrance fee of a shilling, however (double if one purchased the catalogue), put the experience beyond the reach of the poorer classes. A commissioner's report of 1863 suggested that free entrance on a Saturday would make the exhibition available to all, while a higher charge on Mondays would permit those of genteel sensibilities to view the exhibits without being jostled by indiscriminate crowds. These thoughtful suggestions were never implemented.

While O'Neill's picture is perhaps intended to show a cross-section of the R.A.'s typical audience, it more effectively represents a carefully chosen range of recognisable contemporary types, all respectably and neatly dressed, gazing with laudable interest at the 'Picture of the Year'. We cannot, of course, see the picture, but are invited instead to imagine the type of work which has attracted the attentions of the elderly couple, the family group, the supercilious gentleman, the lady equipped with opera glasses and so forth. As was usual, the gallery walls are crowded from floor to ceiling – pictures hung high, or 'skied', would have been virtually invisible, but the work under examination has been accorded an envied place 'on the line' (i.e. at the most convenient viewing level). Its implied popularity has also earned it a barrier of protection from crowds, an honour never accorded to any of O'Neill's own paintings. This scene takes place in a wing of the National Gallery Building in Trafalgar Square, where the R.A. was housed between 1836 and 1869.

Leeds Museums and Galleries (City Art Gallery)

36 The Picture Gallery (1874) (ill. left)
Sir Lawrence Alma-Tadema (1836-1912)
Oil on canvas, 219 x 166 cm
Inscribed *L. Alma Tadema op CXXVI* (above door)

The Dutch-born artist Alma-Tadema provided the later Victorians with an irresistibly detailed version of life in ancient Rome far removed from the academic classicism of his near-contemporary, Lord Leighton. Eschewing mythology and heroism, Alma-Tadema's classical world is peopled by highly naturalistic versions of the Victorians themselves, suitably draped and toga-ed (or, on occasion, rather scandalously undressed) and usually shown in meticulously-researched settings which translate archaeological information into a vision of opulence. Alma-Tadema's paintings often do little more than set up a situation fraught with possible meanings and developments and leave viewers simply to enjoy the scene or to construct their own narrative possibilities. Needless to say, his Romans are a leisured race enjoying as much time to chat, gaze and admire their possessions as the more privileged members of Victorian society might aspire to. Here the pleasures of connoisseurship, viewing a mixture of imported Old Masters and contemporary works in a dealer's gallery, have been transported from Bond Street to Rome, with the obvious implication that the worlds of commerce and art have a long history of interdependence. This work, along with the companion piece, *The Sculpture Gallery* (Hood Museum of Art, New Hampshire) was commissioned by the artist's own dealer, Ernest Gambart, of whom the central standing figure is a lively portrait. His proprietorial gesture shows him to be the owner of the gallery, expounding his wares to an interested audience. The seated woman might be Madame Angelée, Gambart's mistress, and the other men have all been identified as members of the international art market.

On the gallery walls, covered from floor to ceiling in true Victorian fashion, hang Alma-Tadema's versions of the most famous works of the Greeks and Romans, actually known to us only in written descriptions and inferior Pompeiian copies. These noble scenes of sacrifices, heroes and battles, however, are ignored by two spectators who gaze instead at the painting of a lion, 'by the Landseer of the day' as one contemporary critic commented.

Towneley Hall Art Gallery and Museums, Burnley Borough Council

37 The Dutch Cocoa House at the Glasgow International Exhibition (1888) (ill. p.2)
Sir John Lavery (1856-1941)
Oil on canvas, 45.8 x 35.7 cm

Following the success of the Great Exhibition of 1851, Victorian Britain hosted a number of large international displays where the visitor could wander for hours or days among an edifying range of artistic, cultural and trade-related artefacts from across the world. The impact of such exhibitions was not confined to the casual viewer; they involved the building of temporary structures, the sale of catalogues and souvenir merchandise, and the promotion and advertising of the event as a temporary but vital centre for entertainment and socialising as well as self-improvement and aesthetic enjoyment. This emphasis on what we would now term Marketing and Tourism added a note of decided modernity to the rather pedagogic concept of the exhibition as a site for educatonal leisure. In keeping with such modernity, when Glasgow held its International Exhibition at Kelvingrove in 1888, the artist chosen to record the Queen's State Visit to the city and the event was Lavery. He was French-trained and a leading light in the Scottish school, where tonal harmonies, loose handling and excitingly informal compositional arrangements had ousted the lingering traces of Victorian anecdotalism. Lavery virtually became artist-in-residence for the whole exhibition, producing portraits, crowd scenes and depictions of the trade stands and favourite gathering places. Here he shows one of the themed refreshment rooms, a particularly popular feature. Lavery transforms the Dutch Cocoa House, with its deliberately homely display of china and simple furnishings, into an atmospheric essay on colour and light in an inhabited interior, using the positioning and gestures of the figures to convey the sense that a moment of relaxation can be enjoyed here, whilst avoiding any temptation to add an implied narrative or show a range of stereotypical characters.

National Gallery of Scotland, Edinburgh

above:
38. A Study in the National Gallery
Charles Compton

right:
39. Young Woman Drawing a Portrait
Abraham Solomon

38 A Study in the National Gallery (ill. left) (1855)

Charles Compton (1828-84)
Oil on canvas, 25.4 x 30.5 cm
Signed and dated July 1855

The wide-eyed respectful expressions of Compton's three young figures illustrate the growing Victorian conviction that looking at High Art constituted a morally improving pleasure. The object of their gaze is a *Pietà with Mourning Angels* by the Bolognese Renaissance artist, Francesco Francia, which had been purchased by the National Gallery in 1841. It is a religious picture of the kind appreciated as an Old Master but rarely produced by contemporary artists. The two girls respond with quiet seriousness while the boy, equipped with a gallery catalogue, gazes up at some unseen wonder.

The FORBES Magazine Collection, New York

39 Young Woman Drawing a Portrait (1851) (ill. below)

Abraham Solomon (1824-62)
Oil on canvas, 29.2 x 34.4 cm
Signed and dated 1851

Although during Victoria's reign it became increasingly possible for female artists to gain professional status, the lady in Solomon's picture appears to be an amateur in the true sense of the word – she is, quite literally, drawing for love. The lively portrait sketch on her pad indicates that this well-dressed and leisured young lady is suitably accomplished in the art of drawing, but it also permits a more sentimental reading. Her male subject is clearly not present and her abstracted gaze suggests a reverie of imagination or memory. Her situation, seated on a balcony, overlooking a continental landscape, whilst supported by pillows, wrapped in a fur-edged jacket and supplied with the delicacy of grapes, might inform a Victorian audience that she is convalescent and using her artistic skills to focus her reflections on the beloved at home.

The FORBES Magazine Collection

IN THE PUB

40 Rat-catching at the Blue Anchor Tavern, Bunhill Row, Finsbury (c.1850-52)
British School
Oil on canvas, 43 x 53.5 cm

The fact that this rather naively-painted image cannot be attributed to any known professional artist speaks volumes for the status of the activity it shows. This is not an exhibition picture, but a lively account most probably produced for an interested patron (perhaps the owner of the dog, or the landlord of the Tavern). Blood sports of this kind were a hangover from robust eighteenth-century traditions, when all-male audiences could set animals to fight to the death, betting heavily on the results, without the kind of moral opprobrium that developed alongside Victorian sentimentality and respectability. By the mid-nineteenth century cock-fighting and dog-fighting had waned (officially at least) but cock-pits continued to be used for rat-catching, presumably seen as less offensively cruel because rats were classed as vermin. Caught in advance, the rats were loosed into an enclosure where a trained terrier waited to pounce on them. The sport consisted of the number killed in a fixed time. 'Tiny the Wonder', shown here in action, was twice recorded as having despatched two hundred barn rats in under an hour. Though the ambience of vicious bar-room pastimes might suggest a rough, uncultivated audience, they could actually attract betting sportsmen from any walk of life. Fourth from the left in the crowd is Count D'Orsay (1801-1852), formerly a dandy of the Regency period; the year of his death helps date this picture.

On the evidence of Jerome K Jerome's *Three Men in a Boat* of 1889, rat-catching continued as a recognised betting sport throughout the century. Speaking of his dog, the narrator mentions that he '...had learned that the gardener, unknown to myself, had won thirty shillings by backing him to kill rats against time'.

The Museum of London

41 'They talk a power of our Drinking but never think of our Drought' (1862)

Erskine Nicol (1825-1904)
Oil on panel, 18.4 x 25.4 cm
Signed in monogram (bottom right)
Exhibited RSA 1862

One artistic mode whereby low-life tavern scenes were rendered acceptable to Victorian audiences involved formulating them within the conventions of humorous genre. Humour (especially at the expense of uneducated country bumpkins, foreigners or any group which could be identifed as typically different from the painting's intended audience) drew the sting of moral disapprobation, placing work-shy drunkenness safely in the context of anywhere other than urban respectability.

Nicol was born and trained in Scotland and later moved to England, but it was a four-year stay in Ireland and annual return visits that provided the distinctive material for his long, popular series of Irish genre scenes. Needless to say, these pandered to popular conceptions about primitive conditions, lack of sophistication and coarse native tastes. The visual play between the sunny exterior of agricultural labour and the inviting dinginess of the rough rustic bar, plus the lively gestures and expressions, here point up the joke.

Dundee Arts and Heritage (McManus Galleries)

GENTEEL SPORT

42   The Croquet Match (1893)   (ill. below)
Sir John Lavery (1856-1941)
Oil on canvas, 91.5 x 183 cm
Signed
Nottingham only

The dappled sun and shade of an inviting lawn sets the scene for Lavery's atmospheric painting of a leisurely game of croquet. Croquet was a development of the much earlier game of Pall Mall which had virtually died out in England by the eighteenth century, only to reappear in its more modern form in the middle of the nineteenth. Like lawn tennis, part of croquet's appeal was its scale, requiring modest grounds (by the standards of the Victorian gentry) and simple equipment. Also like tennis, it was readily available to purchase – John Jacques and Son, the family firm of sports goods manufacturers, sold sets, including a book of rules, from 1857. The first public championship took place in 1867 and the activity seems to have been attractive to spectators as well as participants. Not so energetic a game as tennis, croquet could be played by enthusiasts of all ages and was considered a sport eminently suitable for ladies. The female figures in Lavery's picture have made few concessions to practicality in their choice of dress but the light, white fabrics and straw hats are seasonably suited to the sunny weather as well as providing a high note in the artist's vibrant colour scheme.

Private Collection

43   The Fair Toxophilites (1872)   (ill. p.11)
William Powell Frith (1819-1909)
Oil on canvas, 98.2 x 81.7 cm
Inscribed *W.P. Frith 1872* (lower left)
Nottingham only

The growing popularity of outdoor sports for young ladies included not only such comparatively novel pursuits as tennis but also those pastimes traditional to country house life such as hunting, shooting and archery. There is a definite air of the aristocratic in Frith's painting with its glimpse of a grand mansion and country estate in the background. The female figures have relinquished little in the way of fashion for the practicalities of their pastime and so can be seen preparing to shoot whilst clad in the *haute couture* of the day, complete with draped skirts, ribbon and lace trimmings and frivolous hats perched on high chignons of hair. Frith's image is less concerned with capturing their enjoyment of the sport than with playing up the dichotomy between the skilled physical activity and the corsetted daintiness of the women who undertake it.

The models were Frith's daughters, Alice, Fanny and Louisa. '...from the waist of the girl on the right hangs a large tassle for cleaning arrows, a greasebox (containing beeswax and lard into which the gloved fingers were dipped), two ornamental acorns and an ivory pencil, probably for scoring.' (Christopher Wood: *Victorian Panorama*, 1976, p.184)

Royal Albert Memorial Museum, Exeter

above:
44. The Lawn Tennis Season
Mary Hayllar

right:
46. A Summer Shower
Edith Hayllar

GENTEEL SPORT

44   The Lawn Tennis Season (1881)   (ill. p.51)
Mary Hayllar (fl.1880-85)
Oil on canvas, 19.3 x 24.3 cm.
Inscribed *Mary Hayllar 1881*

The Hayllar family of artists made a speciality of paintings about comfortable middle-class domestic life which presumably reflected their own family circumstances. This familiarity, combined with an often idiosyncratic attitude towards composition, imparts to their paintings an ease and charm less often found in more formal works. The professional artist James Hayllar seems to have trained all four of his daughters to paint, but although their work was publicly exhibited they continued to live quietly, without direct involvement in the increasingly complex and commercial art world.

With the players reduced to a distant vignette, this painting is actually a domestic still-life focussed on the accoutrements of a game increasingly popular for anyone with a garden large enough to accommodate an *ad hoc* court. Despite the display of racquets, balls and playing shoes, the artist's inclusion of a parasol and light refreshments indicates a mood essentially social rather than competitive.

Southampton City Art Gallery

45   A Summer Shower (1888)

Charles Edward Perugini (1839-1918)
Oil on canvas, 115.5 x 76.5 cm
Signed in monogram (lower right)

In Victorian art, shuttlecock appears as an activity equally suited to adults and children, rude rustic players or genteel young ladies (see cat. no.19). The classicist, Albert Moore, even uses it as a motif in his representations of Greek maidens. Perugini's players, whose game has been interrupted by a shower, are shown wearing the kind of high-waisted neo-classic gowns fashionable at the very beginning of the nineteenth century, thus seeming to represent an historic fancy rather than a scene of contemporary life. However, Aesthetic taste, in conjunction with a growing awareness that heavy, tightly-corsetted outfits were neither the most rational nor attractive mode for the active Victorian woman, had led, by the 1880s, to a revival of less structured garments for the more independent wearer. To a contemporary audience this picture would have combined its nostalgic period charm with the spice of modernity.

Ferens Art Gallery: Kingston upon Hull City Museums, Art Galleries and Archives

46   A Summer Shower (1883)   (ill. p.51)
Edith Hayllar (1860-1948)
Oil on board, 53.3 x 43.2 cm
Inscribed *Edith Hayllar 1883* (lower left)

Edith, second of the Hayllar daughters, produced several paintings which highlight the domestic sports and amusements enjoyed by the family at their home of Castle Priory in Wallingford, Berkshire. Here the chosen game is lawn tennis, a much more accessible variant of Royal (or Real) Tennis which had been patented in 1874 by Major Clopton Wingfield. Its original name of 'Sphairistike', derived from an Homeric term for the ball games of ancient Greece, was, unsurprisingly, rapidly dropped. The game itself, however, proved an instant success, especially with households whose grounds were large enough to house its fairly modest dimensions. The equipment was simple, easily set up and readily available from suppliers – it was possible to purchase the game in a box complete with balls, net and instructions. Its first Code of Rules was published in 1875 by the Marylebone Cricket Club. Tennis was seen as providing healthy exercise and promoting co-ordination without requiring any special training and it could be played privately in the garden at home, as a family recreation or as the focus for a larger social gathering.

In Hayllar's picture the gentle joke is that the activity has been rained off, so the image becomes one of filling in time with enforced repose and desultory conversation in the comfortable informality of a panelled hallway. In the background, lemonade and other refreshments console the would-be players. The female figures wear comparatively short, simple summer dresses for freedom of movement, protected by aprons whose pockets could hold tennis balls. The gentlemen are informally dressed in knickerbockers and stockings with coloured scarves worn as belts.

The FORBES Magazine Collection, New York

right:
45. A Summer Shower
Charles Edward Perugini

CYCLING

above:
48. Repairing the Bicycle
John Quinton Pringle

left:
47. Cycling at Alexandra Palace
CA Fesch

47 Cycling at Alexandra Palace (1886)

CA Fesch

Watercolour on paper, 62.9 x 48 cm

Inscribed *CA Fesch 86*

Although expensive and difficult to ride, the Ordinary bicycle, while in vogue, inspired an accelerating cycle culture of clubs, magazines, races and shops. During the 1880s, amateur clubs were founded across the country, organizing group events and designing their own distinctive uniforms. Cycling was popular as a spectator sport too, with races that could go on for days, and special tracks that attracted a wide range of public viewers, including the important one at Alexandra Palace. This watercolour looks like a highly formalised rendition of a real event – the riders could possibly be portraits, but the stiffly-arranged spectators display a unifom smartness and orderliness which gives no hint of the excited reaction recorded at actual races. The cyclists are wearing specialised track costumes, pared down to the flannel vests and short leggings worn over bare calves, socks and stout but supple footwear. Needless to say, gentlemen amateurs cycling in the public streets would not have adopted this gymnastic form of garb, though some version of the lightweight caps shown might have been acceptable. The conventionally-dressed spectators, of course, wear bowlers and top hats.

The vignettes in the corners show various models of the more sedate contemporary bicycle, obviously viewed as a vehicle for leisurely country outings when compared with the frenetic speed and potential risk proferred by the Ordinary. Top left is a Coventry Rotary tricycle with its distinctive steering handle on the right. Top right is perhaps a Humber Cripper tricycle, bottom left an unidentified variant of the social tricycle that allowed a couple to pedal comfortably side by side. Bottom left is a Humber Tandem, with a small safety wheel in front designed to hit the ground if the trike tipped forward, to prevent the lady being pitched into the road. The portrait roundels must show leading lights in the cycling world, with tentative identification of TR Marriott (top left), CE Liles (top right) and HL Corlis (top centre), the first man to ride twenty miles in the hour. The whole looks less like an exhibition picture and more like the original for a magazine illustratation, or even an advertisement. It has clearly been put together piecemeal using various photographs as sources of visual information.

The Museum of London

48 Repairing the Bicycle (c.1889)

John Quinton Pringle (1864-1925)

Oil on canvas, 30.5 x 45.7 cm

By the middle of the 1880s experiments to design a bicycle more stable than the Ordinary had resulted in several commercially successful 'Safety' cycles of the still-familiar type with two wheels of nearly equal size and a chain to drive the rear wheel. These soon flooded the market, with cheap models bringing cycling within range of a much wider public during the 1890s. They were also taken up by a new generation of more adventurous lady riders in a way that the Ordinary could never have been. Home maintenance became part of the cycling mystique, and Pringle's solitary enthusiast kneels by the garden shed to check the smooth running of his front wheel. Pneumatic tyres (with the concommitant puncture repair kits) had been evolved by JB Dunlop in 1888 and by 1892 were being fitted as standard, but do not seem to be in evidence here. The gentleman's cap and suit represent a typical informal cycling outfit: riders were exhorted to choose practical dark fabrics because of the inevitability of oil stains from the machine.

Glasgow Museums: Art Gallery and Museum, Kelvingrove

49 Lady on a Safety Tricycle (1885)
Sir John Lavery (1856-1941)
Watercolour on paper, 35 x 52 cm
Signed and dated (bottom right and verso)

The cycling craze of the late nineteenth century began slowly in the 1860s with the arrival of the Velocipede or 'Boneshaker' from France. As designs were improved, the front wheel of this machine was expanded in size so the rider no longer had to pedal as quickly and the rear wheel grew smaller to compensate, providing the distinctive silhouette of the Ordinary (or, as it was abusively called, the 'Penny Farthing'). Through the 1870s and early 1880s these provided an exciting (sometimes too much so!) ride for gentlemen enthusiasts and competitors, but were quite unsuitable for female riders. Alongside the Ordinary, however, and almost as popular during the 1880s, were marketed many variations of the Tricycle. These were safer machines, requiring a less precarious (and revealing) perch and reasonably well-suited to feminine fashion, so adventurous ladies might be seen pedalling through the streets – the height of novelty and modernity.

Lavery's French training and the awareness of contemporary continental art which was informing Scottish painting by the 1880s is apparent in the handling of this picture, where the modernity of the motif seems well matched to the uncluttered, atmospheric treatment. The tricycle has no awkward crossbar for the lady to clamber over, but neither does it have handlebars of the modern kind. Instead the rider holds handle grips on either side of her seat and pedals from a comparatively upright position. Divided skirts and bloomers became contentious possibilities for the daring lady cyclist later in the century, but the shape of the tricycle did not demand them and Lavery's figure adopted no special costume beyond a fairly simple skirt, jacket and hat which combine practicality with a fashionable outline. During the late 1880s 'Violet Lorne', writing the Ladies' Column in *Bicycling News*, reminded her readership that:

'It cannot be too often nor too clearly understood by novices of the wheel that a style of costume unlikely to attract attention or remark is the correct wear for the cyclist.'

Government Art Collection

HOLIDAYS

50 Where Next? (ill. p.58)
Edward Frederick Brewtnall (1846-1902)
Watercolour and bodycolour on paper,
18.5 x 28.75 cm
Signed
Nottingham only

The sunny Mediterranean atmosphere, the casual jumble of breakfast things on a table and the easy intimacy of gesture here all bespeak a rather cosmopolitan relaxation much more typical of late Victorian imagery than of anything likely to be depicted earlier in the century. The couple who pore avidly over a map are clearly enjoying the element of exploration possible on a foreign holiday – most probably their honeymoon, for the woman's wedding ring is clearly displayed.

The visual language of the painting encodes the picture-space itself with layers of meaning. The wide expanse of the sea outside and the unfolded map inside imply the unfamiliar territory that the young couple can negotiate with shared enthusiasm and mutual support. At the same time they are depicted at a moment of cosy domesticity, unhurried, informal and at ease with one another. They savour the pleasure of planning their next move, with the implication that the peregrinations of a holiday might stand as model for the journey of life. The viewer is invited to share their interior space, looking out to the landscape beyond, yet at the same time is excluded from their intense personal relationship by the head-to-head pose that hides their eyes and expressions. The careful depiction of the still-life, the recently unfolded tablecloth and the map all indicate that even towards the end of Victoria's reign, the style of the leisure picture could still be deliberately informed by prototypes from Dutch seventeenth-century art.

Private Collection

51 The Children's Holiday (1864) (ill. p.59)
William Holman Hunt (1827-1910)
Oil on canvas, 214 x 147 cm
Inscribed in monogram and dated (lower left corner)

One of the most spectacular of Pre-Raphaelite portraits, this was commissioned from Hunt by Thomas Fairbairn, a collector who already owned two of the artist's earlier works, and was possibly intended to hang at the top of the staircase in his Sussex home, Burton Park. The picture effectively functions as a portrait of the grounds, Mrs Allison Fairbairn, the five youngest Fairbairn children and the family dog. It also includes the full accoutrements of a luxurious tea in the open air, including starched white table cloth, Greek-key tea service and silver tea urn. Mrs Fairbairn's rich satin dress and valuable coral jewellery make this so much an image of conspicuous consumption that it becomes difficult to read its intended function as a document of family affection.

It was painted piecemeal, as and when the various models were available. During its production Mrs Fairbairn was away with her husband on a two-month tour of Europe while Hunt stayed in Sussex attempting to paint the children. Perhaps this accounts for its lack of conviction as an image of a shared occasion. The mother gazes directly outwards as though she was having her photograph taken and with no reference to the children. The eldest boy caresses his dog, a brother and sister have wandered off to feed apples to the deer and in the most appealing group another girl has made a necklace of rosehips for her youngest sibling. The children have obviously been gathering conkers, piled up in the foreground, indicating that this takes place on a mild autumn day. A possible prototype for the theme can be indicated in Van Dyck's seventeenth-century group portrait, *The Five Eldest Children of Charles I.* The Fairbairns actually had seven children and it can be suggested that Constance and Arthur, the two eldest, have been omitted here because they had already been the models for a sculpture group by Thomas Woolner. It is, of course, possible that their being deaf-mutes would have excluded them from the kind of carefree family picnic shown here.

Torre Abbey, Torquay

HOLIDAYS

above:
50. Where Next?
Edward Frederick Brewtnall

right:
51. The Children's Holiday
William Holman Hunt

CHILDREN'S GAMES

52 Ups and Downs (ill. left)
Halbot Knight Browne (1815-92)
Oil on canvas, 59.7 x 39 cm

As 'Phiz', Browne is best known for his illustrations to the novels of Dickens, but his oil paintings indicate a stylish individuality somewhat at odds with contemporary artistic modes. His elongated figures, with their lightly sketched features and fluttering draperies, scarcely belong in the category of detailed naturalistic representation that circumscribes most Victorian images of leisure and possibly his attitude to the subject matter is equally idiosyncratic. Ostensibly this picture shows young people bowling hoops down a hillside on a windy day, but it leaves a suspicion that the 'Ups and Downs' are those of life, not just of the game. The sprightly girls who keep their hoops upright are accompanied by a child, a falling boy and a courting couple, while at the top of the hill an old woman with an umbrella is directed to look across the distant landscape. Some suggestion of the ages of humanity is implicit, but never explained, in this vaguely disturbing grouping of apparently unconnected figures.

Scarborough Borough Council, Department of Tourism and Amenities

53 The Toy Seller (1876) (ill. below)
Mark W Langois (*fl*.1862-73)
(after C Hunt, 1829-1900)
Oil on canvas, 59.5 x 89.5 cm
Signed *C Hunt 76* (bottom right)

Charles Hunt, one of a group of artists profoundly influenced by the cottage scenes of the earlier Scottish painter David Wilkie, specialised in those scenes of tidy rustic domesticity which an urbanised Victorian audience found so reassuring. The fact that this painting is actually a copy after an original by Hunt suggests how popular his work was. The handling has become cruder in the copy but the charm remains. The central figure is actually the woman calmly preparing vegetables while her children respond excitedly to the old pedlar at the door. The implication is that this cosy if humble style of cottage life permits the purchase of such minor luxury items as cheap toys. Mother and toy seller both work, but for the children, play is all important.

Reading Museum Service

54 The Launch (1858)
James Turpin Hart (1835-99)
Oil on canvas, 35.6 x 45.7 cm
Signed *Ja. T. Hart 1858* (bottom right)

The depiction of clean, well-nourished children dressed in decent rustic style and enjoying the simple pleasures of recreation in an idealised Constable-like landscape presented a refreshing (if sanitised) view of rural life for the urbanised Victorian audience. Needing no more elaborate toys than a homemade paper boat, the children's obvious content in their environment presents an idyllic view of unspoiled childhood in harmony with an unspoiled landscape.

City of Nottingham Museums; Castle Museum and Art Gallery

55 Ivanhoe (1871)
Charles Hunt (1829-1900)
Oil on canvas, 74.3 x 113.5 cm
Inscribed *Hunt 1871* (bottom right)

Amongst Hunt's many pictures of children at play is a particularly idiosyncratic group showing *ad hoc* infant dramatisations of famous literary scenes. His paintings of *Macbeth, Hamlet* and *The Merchant of Venice* all actually depict children in fairly bare rustic interiors (possibly suggesting a village school) enthusiastically acting out their roles with an assortment of hastily adapted props and costumes. *Ivanhoe* moves this idea into the world of the historical romance, with a mediaeval tournament fought on furniture for horses while the fair heroine waits to crown the victor. The novels of Sir Walter Scott enjoyed immense popularity with Victorian readers (including Victoria herself) but even so, in order to make the subject of this affectionate parody clear, Hunt has felt obliged to label Ivanhoe and the villain, Bois Guilbert, on their armour and to show two boys reading from a volume of Scott. To the left another child gets into character by having his face painted. While they could be viewed as tributes to the inventiveness of childish imagination, paintings of this kind also displayed a contrived cleverness which has more to do with adult observation and the invitation for the viewer to measure the distance between the children's improvised version of a literary source and the dignity of the real thing.

The FORBES Magazine Collection, New York

CHILDREN'S GAMES

56 The Village Guy Fawkes (1877)
James Lobley (1828-88)
Watercolour on paper, 26.5 x 65 cm
Signed *J Lobley 1877* (bottom right)

Here the annual November the Fifth celebrations are viewed as an occasion for childish excitement, with an *ad hoc* procession attracting even those who, like the apronned boy in the foreground, are already at work. In the backgound to the far right can be glimpsed the preparations for the bonfire on which the guy will be ceremoniously burned, a public festivity which will involve the entire village.

Bradford Art Galleries and Museums

57 Boy with a Guinea Pig (1864)
John Joseph Barker (*fl.*1835-66)
Oil on canvas, 30.2 x 25.3 cm
Signed *JJ Barker/1864* (lower left)

A scene not so much of poverty as of rural simplicity, this painting is very old fashioned in its handling for 1864, with a mass of generalised feathery foliage which eschews any influence of Pre-Raphaelite precision. The figures of the three children are equally generalised in their appeal – these are gentle country children (one wears a smock) and despite the bare feet of the seated boy they do not look ill-fed or neglected. Indeed, the picture is about having time and inclination to care for a pet even when life is lived at a very simple level of material well-being. The guinea pig, enjoying an airing, has been carried around in what appears to be a convenient homemade hutch equipped with a strap worn round its young owner's neck. The suggestion must be that he habitually carries his beloved pet with him.

Victoria Art Gallery; Bath and North East Somerset Council

right:
57. Boy with a Guinea Pig
John Joseph Barker

PETS

above:
56. The Village Guy Fawkes
James Lobley

right:
58. Puss in Boots
Sir John Everett Millais

58 Puss in Boots (1877) (ill. p.65)
Sir John Everett Millais (1829-96)
Oil on canvas, 106.7 x 79.3 cm
Signed in monogram (bottom left)

Although he began his career as a member of the Pre-Raphaelite Brotherhood, by the 1860s Millais had effectively jettisoned precision of detail and seriousness of subject in favour of more rapidly produced paintings designed to appeal to popular taste. Sentimental images of attractive children came to figure large in his output, the most famous being *Bubbles,* an image subsequently used to advertise Pear's soap.

Puss in Boots represents a bravura example of Millais' fluid brushwork employed on a subject of pampered childhood leisure which seems to be little more than a play on a trite and appealing title. The pet cat is obviously as docile as the doll who has contributed its knitted bootees to the game. The child, however, for all her pinafored, golden-curled beauty, has a knowing expression which seems to betray the sense of control informing her relationship with cat and doll alike.

Dundee Arts and Heritage (McManus Galleries)

59 For a Good Boy (1880)
Mary Hayllar (*fl.*1880-85)
Oil on board, 40.6 x 29.2 cm
Inscribed *Mary Hayllar 1880* (bottom left)

Mary Hayllar's painting, which was exhibited at the Royal Academy, plays with a favourite compositional device of simultaneously inviting us to absorb the atmosphere of an interior while giving us a vista of what lies outside. The view through the window, with its leafy walk and rustic seat, suggests the pleasure of a turn in the open air after the ritual of afternoon tea. Meanwhile the lady amuses herself by putting her little dog through his paces begging for titbits.

The FORBES Magazine Collection, New York

right:
59. For a Good Boy
Mary Hayllar

THE PARLOUR GAMES TABLE

60 The Card Party (1898) (ill. p.68)
Sir Alfred J Munnings (1878-1959)
Pencil monochrome watercolour on paper, frame
painted in oils, 22 x 31.1 cm
Signed *A.J. Munnings -98-* (lower left)

Despite stern moral strictures against gambling, the
Victorians accepted and developed the tradition of card
playing as a suitable pastime both for family entertainment
and for more formal occasions. The after-dinner round of
cards often represented a cherished part of household
routine which different generations could enjoy together.

In this curiously personal little artefact, where the
decorated frame is themed to match the image it encloses,
Munnings reveals his Victorian roots. Despite being
produced so late in the century, its air of cosy domesticity
and conversational subtitle of *Whist, One More Round* still
reflect unchallenged assumptions of iconography and
composition. Munnings went on to become President of
the Royal Academy and in post-war Britain made a
controversially traditionalist stand against artistic
modernism.

Norfolk Museums Service (Norwich Castle Museum)

61 A Game of Cards (1890s) (ill. p.68)
Nancy A Sabine Pasley (*fl.*1886-92)
Oil on canvas, 19.2 x 29.5 cm
Signed *NA Sabine Pasley* (lower left)

Little is known about this London-based female artist and
it is tempting to assume that the painting shows her own
home, perhaps with members of her family as the sitters.
The sitting room looks like a loving depiction of a real
place, complete with potted plant, overmantle mirror and
the range of pictures, ornaments and knick-knacks that
accumulate over years of family occupation. The little
green-topped card table, here conveniently placed
between chaise longue and upright chair, indicates the
players' pastime to be a favourite one for which they are
comfortably equipped.

Geffrye Museum, London

62 Experientia Docet (1884) (ill. p.69)
Walter Dendy Sadler (1854-1923)
Oil on canvas, 76.4 x 110.8 cm
Signed *W Dendy Sadler 84* (bottom left)

Sadler's gently humorous or sentimental genre scenes
represent favourite Victorian themes which gave an
additional appeal by being set in unfamiliar circumstances.
He particularly favoured eighteenth- and early nineteenth-
century contexts for his little dramas of human nature, yet
it is difficult to see the players as anything other than
Victorian. A sub-genre Sadler virtually created was the
mildly satirical scene of clerical or monastic life. Here, in
a well-appointed interior, three priests engage in the
delightfully innocent worldliness of a game of cards over
their tea or coffee, indicating the universal appeal of trivial
leisure-time pursuits even where some more elevated
occupation might have been looked for. The contemporary
popularity of Sadler's pictures is indicated by their frequent
reproduction, but he has not yet been rediscovered by
modern taste.

Rochdale Art Gallery Collection

63 The Chess Players. The Lonsdale Family (ill. p.69)
James Lonsdale (1777-1839)
Oil on canvas, 142.2 x 111.8 cm
Exeter only

A painter of Regency portraits rather than the Victorian
genre, Lonsdale is represented here because this late work
functions as an interesting precursor to the 'leisure portrait'
that became popular later in the century. Despite its genre-
like title and the 'gentleman's club' atmosphere of its all-
male group intent on their game, the painting should be
read as a proud and affectionate paternal tribute to the
intellectual prowess of its sitters, the artist's three sons.
Recent research identifies them as Richard Lonsdale
(seated, wearing smoking cap), himself an artist; James John
(standing, holding hookah pipe), Recorder of Folkestone,
and Edward Francis, founder of and surgeon at the Royal
Orthopaedic Hospital. The older, bespectacled figure at the
back is a self-portrait of the painter, slightly detached from
the three brothers whose fraternal links are emphasised by
their shared concentration on this game of calculation,
foresight and pitted wits.

City of Nottingham Museums; Castle Museum and Art Gallery

above:
61. A Game of Cards
Nancy A Sabine Pasley

right:
60. The Card Party
Sir Alfred J Munnings

68   The Pursuit of Leisure

above:
62. Experientia Docet
Walter Dendy Sadler

right:
63. The Chess Players. The Lonsdale Family
James Lonsdale

64 Hearts are Trumps (1872)
Sir John Everett Millais (1829-96)
Oil on canvas 165.7 x 219.7 cm
Signed and dated *JM 1872* (lower left)

Millais was at the height of his popularity as a society portrait painter when the inventor and industrialist Sir William Armstrong commissioned from him an elaborate portrait of his daughters, Elizabeth, Diana and Mary, with price no object. This commission permitted Millais to prove a point: a recent review of his work had, while admitting his mastery in most branches of his art, bewailed the fact that he would find it impossible to create a successful portrait of three beautiful women in contemporary dress in the way that Sir Joshua Reynolds had done in 1781, with his *Three Ladies Waldegrave*. Millais knew this work (now in the National Gallery of Scotland, but then belonging to Frances, Countess of Waldegrave, at Strawberry Hill) and set out to paint a modern equivalent. Far from avoiding the

elaboration of fashionable dress in the 1870s, he actually designed his sitters' opulent grey gowns trimmed with lace and pink satin whose shimmering subtleties of tone are obviously meant to evoke the work of Velasquez.

Reynolds' triple portrait had shown three aristocratic sisters embroidering and winding silk thread. Millais' similarly grouped Victorian damsels, the daughters of a self-made man, play dummy whist instead, and the one on the right even involves us in the game by sharing her hand with us. The painting, shown in 1878 at the *Exposition Universelle* in Paris, proved a great critical success, with favourable comment not only on the English-rose beauty of the girls, but also on the handling of the Chinese screen, inlaid card table and azaleas. The title implies romance as well as relating to the game, but it remains unclear whether it was sitters or artist who selected whist as a suitable activity.

Tate Gallery. Presented by the Trustees of the Chantrey Bequest, 1945

TRANQUIL HOURS

65 A Quiet Half Hour (1876)
Lionel Charles Henley (c.1843-93)
Oil on panel, 22.9 x 17.5 cm

Small images of attractive figures (usually female) doing very little, but doing it with a certain charm in an appropriate setting, can represent to modern eyes one of the most enigmatic facets of Victorian genre painting. With an emphasis on fashion, coiffure and accessories, plus an absence of any strong narrative implication, the temptation is to read these as portraits; but where the sitter is an appealing 'type' rather than a named individual, this remains inappropriate. Such works function as 'fancy pictures' even where they utilise a portrait format. Sometimes the background is as important as the figures, and the pictures play variations on those Dutch seventeenth-century interiors where the naturalistic depiction of a room complete with furnishings and inhabitants provided sufficient visual material to satisfy the taste of middle-class domestic patrons avid for the recognisable rather than the intellectual.

In Henley's picture the relaxed pose of the woman, feet up before the fire, as, following afternoon tea, she enjoys an amusing read, is sufficiently informal to ensure the work's identity as genre rather than portrait. Despite fashionable blue and white china and a Japanese screen whose pattern of cranes and fans would delight the Aesthetic taste of the 1870s, the atmosphere is one of cosiness and warmth, emphasised by the unselfconscious way the figure leans back into her light cane chair. The ruched edging of her dress was very fashionable in the '70s, but its apparently unstructured skirt strikes an odd note in the context of mid-decade bustles and overskirts drawn back into complex elaborations of folds and trimmings. The one time of the social day, however, when a lady might relax sartorial etiquette by wearing a looser (possibly even uncorsetted) outfit was at teatime, before dressing for dinner – a reference which a contemporary audience might well have inferred from this image.

Hinton Ampner, The Ralph Ditton Collection (The National Trust)

66 Portrait of Mrs Walker (1860s) (ill. p.71)
Valentine Cameron Prinsep (1838-1904)
Oil on canvas, 135 x 104 cm

Unlike Henley's *A Quiet Half Hour* (cat. no. 65), where the figure merely represents a generalised notion of a leisured lady, this image was commissioned as a portrait of a specific sitter who presumably contributed to the choice of motif, electing to have herself shown gazing up from the knitting which she holds on her lap.

Bury Art Gallery and Museum

67 Lady with Japanese Screen and Goldfish (Portrait of the artist's mother) (1886)
James Cadenhead (1858-1927)
Oil on canvas, 119 x 187 cm (framed)
Signed *James Cadenhead 1886* (bottom left)
Nottingham only
Illustrated in colour on back cover

The sitter here is not shown in elaborate fashionable dress but wearing the sort of severe black gown associated with mourning and deemed especially suitable for older women. Its unrelieved darkness, however, is used by the artist as a visual foil for the harmony of golds, oranges and yellows which constitute the painting's main charm and which, in conjunction with the exoticism of the Japanese screen, suggests the influence of Whistler. The goldfish add a further note of orientalism, indicating the kind of tastefully artistic lifestyle this composed lady enjoys. Just as her son has arranged the toning colours of the painting, she is comparing a selection of russet and golden embroidery silks for the fine needlework which is obviously her hobby.

City Art Centre, Edinburgh

page 71:
66. Portrait of Mrs Walker
Valentine Cameron Prinsep

above:
67. Lady with Japanese Screen and Goldfish
(Portrait of the artist's mother)
James Cadenhead

right:
65. A Quiet Half Hour
Lionel Charles Henley

68 Interior: Girl Reading (1875)
Alfred Provis (fl.1843-86)
Oil on panel, 23.2 x 31.8 cm
Signed on frame A. Provis. 1875

Provis specialised in small detailed interiors of cottages and farmhouses, but whereas most of these show figures involved in domestic chores, here a young girl finds a tranquil moment to read her book, which by its size can be most readily identified as the family bible. Indeed, with its shadowed interior and warm luminosity centred on the girl and her dog, this picture draws on Dutch seventeenth-century traditions of realism, a reference which informs the humble figure with a resonant seriousness of intention. Although her setting represents an unglamorised version of cottage life, the throne-like carved chair before which she sits on a low stool introduces a curious visual disjunction. It is presumably an old-fashioned piece abandoned from the 'grand house', but in this context it reinforces a gravity of suggestion that goes beyond the simple subject.

Ferens Art Gallery: Kingston upon Hull City Museums, Art Galleries and Archives

69 Young Woman Reading in an Attic Bedroom (1861)

Alice Squire (1840-1936)

Watercolour with pen and ink over pencil,
14.2 x 20.5 cm
Signed *Alice Squire*
Separately inscribed *Painted in 1861*

A member of the *Society of Lady Artists*, Alice Squire was a London painter of genre and landscape. This peaceful watercolour has sometimes been known by the title *The Governess* but there is little internal evidence to suggest that this is the figure's status. She is quietly reading alongside her sleeping cat in a neat attic bedroom and while her primly modest appearance and unpretentious surroundings might not suggest a life of luxury, neither do they necessarily convey the privations of a governess's domestic circumstances. In fact, the room is redolent of comfort and convenience and the lady seems entirely at home in it. It is personalised to the extent that not only her bonnet, umbrella and correspondence are shown but also the idiosyncratic touch of fronds of seaweed hung before the window, presumably as a means of predicting the weather.

Geffrye Museum, London

MUSICAL PLEASURES

70 A Philharmonic Rehearsal in a Farmhouse (1860)
(ill. below)

John Evan Hodgson (1831-95)
Oil on canvas, 85 x 110 cm
Signed *J.E. Hodgson 1860*

Philharmonic Societies were informal musical groups, effectively amateur bands or orchestras, which practised together in any available space in preparation for local concerts and other social events. Hodgson's picture depicts a group of musicians rehearsing Handel's *Israel in Egypt* amongst the family occupations of a cottage interior. They represent an interesting social mix, a cross-section of village life, including artisans and well-to-do professional gentlemen. The picture, not without a touch of humour in its implied incongruity, suggests that high culture was potentially within the reach of all and could flourish in the humble surroundings of an English yeoman's dwelling.

Wolverhampton Art Gallery and Museums

71 The Music Lesson
(ill. p.78)

Frederick Walker (1840-75)
Watercolour on paper, 14 x 19 cm
Signed with initials (lower right)

Despite its title this mildly humorous watercolour actually shows informal music-making at home, to which the child is an interested party and where the level of enthusiasm may perhaps outweigh that of accomplishment. The candle-lit piano and the tea-cup on the table add to the air of domesticity. The well-captured expression of the man's face is a reminder that Walker was a popular illustrator, skilled in conveying the nuances of a situation. Although he also painted in oils, his fresh and lively watercolours (more typically of rural subjects) represent the most characteristic and attractive part of his output.

Bury Art Gallery and Museum

above:
71. The Music Lesson
Frederick Walker

right:
73. The Dancing Platform
at Cremorne Gardens
Phoebus Levin

far right:
75. Spring Moonlight
John Henry Lorimer

72 Mrs John Pettie, 1865 (ill. p.76)
by Sir William Quiller Orchardson (1832-1910)
Oil on canvas, 99.9 x 79.5 cm

This picture functions as an affectionate testament to the close friendship, both professional and personal, that flourished between the artists, Orchardson and Pettie. The portrait of the latter's wife, painted as a wedding gift, draws attention to her intense, solemn expression and slender, sensitive hands as she plays the piano. This is not the image of fashionplate prettiness one might expect of a Victorian bride, but shows her as absorbed in her own musical accomplishment.

Manchester City Art Galleries

73 The Dancing Platform at Cremorne Gardens (1864) (ill. p.78)
Phoebus Levin (fl.1836-78)
Oil on canvas, 66.2 x 107.5 cm
Signed *P. Levin 1864*

Between 1846 and 1877 the grounds of Cremorne House were open to the public as Pleasure Gardens, somewhat on the eighteenth-century model of Vauxhall. For the entrance fee of one shilling one could enjoy fireworks, concerts, balloon ascents, vaudeville and especially dancing. As this effervescent mixture might suggest, the Gardens were popular rather than exclusive, enjoying a reputation that ranged from the raffish to the downright riotous. The lively scene shown here manages to suggest an atmosphere more sociable than respectable, despite its emphasis on high fashion and elegance. Inside the dancing platform with its central pagoda, couples dance, while the orchestra plays and other customers stroll or sit at tables amongst the trees. Perhaps the exaggerated crinoline and the glimpse of ankle seen on the woman seated on the right would indicate to a contemporary audience that the Garden might be a venue for illicit liaisons.

The Museum of London

74 The Music Party
Alfred Tidey (1808-92)
Watercolour, 49.5 x 59.5 cm
Inscribed in monogram (bottom right)

The performance of suitable music in the home constituted not only a useful social accomplishment but a genuine pleasure both within the family circle and for more formal evening entertainments. In this panelled room with its sense of solid luxury, we are shown only the performers and we ourselves fulfil the role of audience. We are effectively being asked to imagine the music played. The women are fashionably gowned, but as they wear long-sleeved day dresses rather than evening dresses this would not appear to be an after-dinner entertainment. Indeed, despite the unavoidably deliberate posture of the woman with the harp, the group of girls round the piano conveys a feeling of spontaneity, of sisters joining in an impromptu rendition. The figures are reputed to be portraits of members of the Abell family.

Worthing Museum and Art Gallery

75 Spring Moonlight (1896) (ill. p.79)
John Henry Lorimer (1856-1936)
Oil on canvas, 183 x 130 cm

Lorimer's training at the RSA under William McTaggart, as well as his time in Paris, become evident in the light handling and luminous effects of this scene, where the Great Hall at Kellie Castle (his family home) is the setting for spontaneous domestic music-making. Despite its original title of *The Dance*, used when it was shown at the RA in 1897, the painting does not depict the social ritual of a formal event, but imagines a moment when the mood of a spring evening invites the young mother to whirl around, her baby in her arms, to the accompaniment of a smiling friend at the piano. The child's nurse, of course, does not join in the moment of affectionate jollity but waits in a corner to take the infant to bed.

Kirkcaldy Museum and Art Gallery

above:
74. The Music Party
Alfred Tidey

FAMILY PARTIES

76 Baby's Birthday (1867)
Frederick Daniel Hardy (1826-1911)
Oil on canvas, 65 x 90 cm
Signed *F.D. Hardy 1867*

The celebration of birthdays and anniversaries was increasingly emphasised as part of family life, providing a focus for the approved sentimentality about relationships, children and 'Home-Sweet-Home'. Hardy imagines a household of simple tastes but modest prosperity and obvious affection. Amid the cheery clutter of a room which combines workshop (the sewing paraphernalia on the left), kitchen (food to warm by the range on the right) and dining room, a family of five children gather around a table to celebrate the first birthday of the youngest. Mother makes the tea, father greets the adoring grandparents and even the family cat gets involved in the warmth of the occasion. The miniature flag which adorns the birthday cake, and the glimpse of the local church tower, indicate patriotism and piety as foundations for such reassuring domestic harmony.

Wolverhampton Art Gallery and Museums

77 Many Happy Returns of the Day (1856)
William Powell Frith (1819-1909)
Oil on canvas, 81.5 x 114.5 cm
Inscribed: *WP Frith 1856* (bottom right)
Exeter only

By contrast with the Hardy, Frith's picture of a baby's first birthday party depicts a family tea of some luxury. The presence of a pretty maid-servant carrying birthday gifts emphasises the fact that this is a distinctly prosperous middle-class household. The child is be-ribboned, garlanded and seated beneath a hoop of greenery which adds an ostentatious air of occasion. Some cordial is being dispensed from decanters and drunk from fine glasses, and

it is difficult to avoid the suspicion that this is sherry, eminently suitable for a celebratory toast, but unexpected in the hands of children. Like Hardy's *Baby's Birthday* (cat. no.76), the picture stresses family unity across the generations, with Grandfather seated in an easy chair in the foreground receiving his glass from a dutiful grandchild under the careful eye of her doting father. To some extent this picture relates to Frith's own family, for Papa is a self-portrait, Grandmama seated at the opposite end of the table is his mother and the birthday girl is one of his daughters. It remains a carefully concocted, idealised composition, however, rather than a representation of any real event: the model for the Grandfather was a suitably venerable-looking old man from the Workhouse.

The Mercer Art Gallery, Harrogate Museum and Arts

78 The Wedding Breakfast (1871) (ill. p.84-85)

Frederick Daniel Hardy (1826-1911)
Oil on canvas, 95 x 131 cm
Inscribed *F.D. Hardy. 1871* (bottom right)

Like birthdays, weddings presented the Victorian artist with the opportunity to construct an idealised version of family life centred around one of its rites of passage. While paintings of courtship usually centred on the romantic relationship of a young couple, images of weddings were more likely to emphasise a shared social occasion which brought together an extended family in a mood both celebratory and sentimental. The best known example is probably Hick's *Changing Homes* (Geffrye Museum), but Hardy's painting presents a more homely view of the wedding breakfast as a domestic ritual which brings together the bridal party in the relaxed atmosphere of their own home. The surroundings are far from grand, although everyone looks healthy and prosperous in their Sunday best. The household obviously employs at least two maidservants and has a pair of ancestral portraits hanging on the wall, yet the dining room has a flagged floor. Perhaps this is a farming family, comfortable but old-fashioned and practical in the style of its surroundings. Only the immediate family is seated at the table, but through the door a servant is pouring ale for a couple of additional wellwishers, perhaps some farm workers of a slightly different class. Those seated at the table drink wine from more delicate glasses and anticipate the cutting of an elaborate flower-trimmed wedding cake.

Sefton MBC Leisure Services Department, Arts and Cultural Services Section, the Atkinson Art Gallery, Southport

79 Dinner at Haddo House (1884)

Alfred Edward Emslie (b.1848, *fl.*1867-89)
Oil on canvas, 36.8 x 57.8 cm
Signed *AE Emslie* (lower left)

While the simple pleasures of home life in some suitably picturesque cottage permitted endless Victorian variations on the uncomplicated sentimentality of 'Home-Sweet-Home,' images of domestic harmony amongst the rich proved rather more problematic. A satirical or moral edge often implied that fashionable life was fraught with tension, but the function of this example as a group portrait of recognisable sitters steers it clear of any such implications. Despite the self-conscious modernity of its viewpoint and arrangement, the picture bears a debt to those eighteenth-century conversation-pieces which record a plausible gathering for its own sake without inviting anecdotal interpretation. The setting is a dinner party at Haddo House in Scotland where a piper in Highland dress is about to pipe in the dessert. The well-dressed company, lavish table setting and richly furnished room bespeak a formality which the composition itself helps to undercut; this is not a state occasion but merely (the painting suggests) the way things are done in the best houses. In the foreground, the Marchioness of Aberdeen is shown with her back to the viewer and in *profile perdue*, a rather informal presentation of so aristocratic a hostess which, together with the briskness of Emslie's handling, indicates that this painting would have looked decidedly modern in relation to the more conscious arrangement of earlier Victorian portraits. To her right the artist has managed to isolate the distinctive profile of Prime Minister Gladstone, visiting his Midlothian constituency. A future prime minister, Lord Rosebery, sits to the left beside Lady Harriet Lindsay.

National Portrait Gallery

above:
79. Dinner at Haddo House
Alfred Edward Emslie

THE MORAL DIMENSION

above:
81. Early Sorrow
Frederick Daniel Hardy

80 For Sale (1857) (ill. p.91)
James Collinson (1825-81)
Oil on canvas, 58.4 x 45.7 cm

Collinson is perhaps the least well-known member of the original Pre-Raphaelite Brotherhood, having a comparatively short and undistinguished career as a professional artist. Despite its straightforward descriptive subject and the conventional, fashionplate prettiness of its female figure, the style of this picture still indicates something of the relentless emphasis on highly-realised details which characterised early Pre-Raphaelitism.

The subject is a charity bazaar selling the kind of elaborately crafted decorative items produced by the daughters of prosperous families as a way of filling leisure time and discharging their social responsibilities. There could be a satirical implication here, that good works intended for the relief of the poor find their expression in the idle production of such unnecessary items as the decorated braces, glass-protected wax flowers and beaded purse, all depicted with such loving precision. It is possible that the title also reflects on the young lady herself, using the occasion to display both the fruits of her labour and the elegant finery which contribute to her prospects on the marriage market.

City of Nottingham Museums; Castle Museum and Art Gallery

81 Early Sorrow (1861) (ill. left)
Frederick Daniel Hardy (1826-1911)
Oil on canvas, 21.6 x 34.3 cm
signed *F.D. Hardy 1861* (top centre)

This variation on *Who killed Cock Robin?* depicts cottage children play-acting the ritual of a formal funeral for their pet bird whose empty cage can be seen to the left. Father looks up from his work mending shoes and mother from her sewing to display sympathetic interest in a game that is also a sad reality. The solemnity of the mock cortège, with the girls ostentatiously black-veiled and weeping and the young gravedigger waiting outside, permits this to function as a satirical comment on the elaboration of adult funerals, yet the title indicates the possibility of real grief. The avid interest of the household cat in the right-hand corner adds a suggestive humorous touch.

Towneley Hall Art Gallery and Museums, Burnley Borough Council

82 The Last Day of the Sale (1857) (ill. p.90)
George Bernard O'Neill (1828-1917)
Oil on canvas, 73.6 x 113 cm
Artist's name appears in the open sale catalogue on table (right foreground). Inscribed on reverse *Painted by G.B. O'Neill 1857, no.1 the last day of the Sale.*

In some Victorian representations the iconography of leisure becomes heavily encoded with moral messages whereby the artist indicates that a 'neutral' reading of the subject as purely descriptive is inappropriate to the intention. 'Good' leisure themes tend to the philanthropic and high-minded – charity work, self-improvement, dignified public occasions – while 'bad' examples show the misuse of time and energy on wasteful or vicious pursuits.

While *The Last Day of the Sale* does not occupy such undisputed moral terrain, still O'Neill's choice of treatment of motifs plays on the notion that the breaking up of a household can proffer the dubious entertainment of prying inspection and cupidinous bargain-hunting. Whilst the auctioneer's audience clearly enjoys the occasion in an almost theatrical way, their attitudes scarcely show human nature at its most attractive.

Towneley Hall Art Gallery and Museums, Burnley Borough Council

above:
82. The Last Day of the Sale
George Bernard O'Neill

far right:
80. For Sale
James Collinson

90 The Pursuit of Leisure

83 The Night School (1892) (ill. below)
Edgar Bundy (1862-1922)
Oil on canvas, 94.2 x 153.6 cm
Signed *Edgar Bundy, 1892* (lower right)

Although the Education Act of 1870 had provided Britain with a system of national schools, there continued to flourish a tradition of evening schools, often staffed by volunteers, which allowed working men to further their education in their spare time. Although not strictly speaking a leisure activity, this process certainly occupied leisure time at the end of a working day and Bundy's atmospheric painting uses pose, expression and lighting to convey the intensity of purpose that fills the shabby room. Most of the adult pupils are reading, but the young man in the foreground sits with furrowed brow over a page of geometric drawings, his compasses neglected before him. Attention is drawn to his large, work-roughened hands as he drums his fingers on the table, isolated from his companions by his introspective attitude. Despite the mild humour of the man on the right who puzzles over his book, the intention here seems far from satirical, so the central figure's expression conveys not mental incapacity but a concentration that goes beyond the mathematical problem he is solving.

Ferens Art Gallery, Kingston upon Hull City Museums, Art Galleries and Archives

84 The Gambler's Wife (1897) (ill. right)
by Margaret Murray Cookesley
(*fl.*1884-1910, d.1927)
Oil on canvas, 149.8 x 105.4 cm
Inscribed *M. Murray Cookesley 1897* (bottom right)
Exeter only

Although it depicts the accoutrements of what could have been a fashionably elegant evening party, both the title of this picture and the melodramatic pose of its single figure leave no doubt concerning its moralising intention. The overturned glass and scattered cards indicate a game that went on too long, leaving traces of chaos suggestive of at least one player's despair. The gambler's wife, a stately figure dressed in Empire fashion, faces the light of dawn with an attitude of painful realisation that the previous night's gaming must now be paid for.

Towneley Hall Art Galleries and Museum, Burnley Borough Council

85 The Opening Ceremony of the Great Exhibition (1851)

(ill. left)

James Digman Wingfield (fl.1832-72)
Oil on canvas, 139.7 x 106.7 cm

The apogee of Victorian high-mindedness concerning edifying amusement was the Great Exhibition of 1851. Largely the brainchild of the Prince Consort, this was a huge international display of materials and manufactured goods from across the globe, housed in Hyde Park in the 'Crystal Palace' designed by Paxton. The building, with its glass skin supported by iron columns and girders, represented a remarkable feat of contemporary engineering and was itself a major attraction. Once inside, however, the visitors who flocked from all parts of the kingdom could roam through hall upon hall of artefacts, machinery and curiosities, absorbing the unspoken message that these fruits of industry, trade and commerce represented a tribute to Britain's role as a world power. Special day excursions to see the Exhibition ran from any location within range, and provincial families took holidays in London just to explore this once-in-a-lifetime display of wonders. A day at the Exhibition must have been equally exhausting to minds, eyes and feet, and refreshment rooms offered a necessary respite from the intensive absorbtion of information.

Wingfield's painting shows the Opening Ceremony, complete with well-behaved crowds around the podium and fountain and thronging the gallery. Recognisable dignitaries include the Queen and Prince Consort, the Duke of Wellington and the Archbishop of Canterbury, but the emphasis is less on their roles than on the sheer scale of the building, emphasised by the mature elm trees on the site which were deliberately enclosed within the structure, suggesting that even Nature could be incorporated into the most elevating and useful of displays.

City of Nottingham Museums; Castle Museum and Art Gallery

Select Bibliography

Becker, Edwin (ed.), *Sir Lawrence Alma-Tadema*, Van Gogh Museum, Amsterdam / Walker Art Gallery, Liverpool 1996

Beevers, David (ed.), *Brighton Revealed*, Brighton Art Gallery, 1995

Bennet, Mary, *Millais*, Walker Art Gallery, Liverpool / RA London 1967

Cowling, Mary, *The Artist as Anthropologist*, Cambridge 1989

Gillet, Paula, *The Victorian Painter's World*, Alan Sutton Publishing Ltd, Gloucester 1990

Ginsberg, Madeleine, *Victorian Dress in Photographs*, Batsford, London 1982

Hogarth, Paul, *Arthur Boyd Houghton*, V&A, London 1975

Matyjaszkiewicz, Krystyna, *James Tissot*, Barbican / Phaidon 1984

Newall, Christopher, *Victorian Watercolours*, Phaidon, Oxford 1987

Noakes, Aubrey, *William Frith, Extraordinary Victorian Painter*, Jupiter, London 1978

Lionel Lambourne and Patricia Connor, *Derby Day 200*, RA London 1979

Simon, Robin and Smart, Alastair, *John Player Art of Cricket*, Secker and Warburg 1983

Treuherz, *Julian Victorian Painting*, Thames and Hudson, London 1993

Tullie House Museum and Art Gallery (gallery pamphlet), *Sam Bough: The Life of a Carlisle Artist*, Carlisle

Wingfield, Mary Ann, *Sport and the Artist Vol I. 'Ball Games'*, Antique Collectors Club, Woodbridge, Suffolk 1988

Wood, Christopher, *Dictionary of Victorian Painters* (2 vols), revised edition, Antique Collectors Club, Woodbridge, Suffolk 1995

Wood, Christopher, *Paradise Lost*, Trafalgar Square Publishing, Vermont 1989

Wood, Christopher, *Victorian Painting*, Antique Collectors Club, Woodbridge, Suffolk 1996

Wood, Christopher, *Victorian Panorama*, Faber and Faber, London 1976

Photographic acknowledgements

Alfred East Art Gallery, Kettering: cat. no.16; © Ashmolean Museum, Oxford: cat. nos.10, 30; Atkinson Art Gallery / Bridgeman Art Library: cat. nos.21, 78; © Birmingham Museums and Art Gallery: cat. nos.15, 28; Bradford Art Galleries and Museums: cat. no.56; Bury Art Gallery and Museum: cat. nos.66, 71; City Art Centre, Edinburgh: cat. no.67; City Museum and Art Gallery, Stoke on Trent: cat. no.29; City of Nottingham Museums; Castle Museum and Art Gallery: cat. nos.31, 34, 54, 63, 80, 85; Dundee Arts and Heritage (McManus Galleries): cat. nos.9, 41, 58; Ferens Art Gallery: Kingston upon Hull City Museums, Art Galleries and Archives: cat. nos.45, 68, 83; Geffrye Museum, London E2: cat. nos.61, 69; Glasgow Museums: Art Gallery and Museum, Kelvingrove: cat. nos.19,48; © Crown copyright: UK Government Art Collection: cat. nos.2, 49; reproduced by kind permission of the Harris Museum and Art Gallery, Preston: cat. no.33; Mathew Hollow: cat. no.42; Kirkcaldy Museum and Art Gallery: cat. no.75; Laing Art Gallery, Newcastle upon Tyne (Tyne & Wear Museums): cat. no.23; Leeds Museums and Galleries: cat. nos.11,35; © Manchester City Art Galleries: cat. no.72; MCC: cat. no.27; MCC / Bridgeman Art Library: cat. no.26; by courtesy of the National Portrait Gallery, London: cat. no.79; Norfolk Museums Service (Norwich Castle Museum): cat. nos.5, 60; Norfolk Museums Service (Thetford Ancient House Museum): cat. no.7; Private collection, courtesy of the Christopher Wood Gallery: cat. no.50; Royal Albert Memorial Museum, Exeter: cat. no.43; Reading Museum Service (Reading Borough Council): cat no.53; Rochdale Art Gallery: cat. no.62; Royal Pavilion, Art Gallery and Museums, Brighton and Hove: cat. nos.13, 14; Russell-Cotes Art Gallery and Museum / Bridgeman Art Library: cat. no.1; Scarborough Borough Council, Department of Tourism and Leisure Services, Scarborough Art Gallery: cat. no.52; Southampton City Art Gallery: cat. no.44; © Tate Gallery, London: cat. nos.4,17; Tate Gallery, London: cat. nos.25, 64; The FORBES Magazine Collection, New York, All Rights Reserved: cat. nos.32, 38, 39, 46, 55, 59; The Mercer, Harrogate / Bridgeman Art Library: cat. no.77; The Museum of London: cat. nos.40, 47, 73; The National Gallery of Scotland: cat. nos.20, 37; The National Trust Photographic Library/Christopher Hurst: cat. no.65; Torre Abbey, Torquay: cat. no.51; Towneley Hall Art Gallery and Museum, Burnley Borough Council: cat. no.36, 84; Towneley Hall Art Gallery and Museum, Burnley Borough Council/Bridgeman Art Library: cat. nos.22, 81, 82; Tullie House Museum and Art Gallery, Carlisle: cat. no.24; Victoria Art Gallery; Bath & North East Somerset Council: cat. nos.8, 57; Wolverhampton Art Gallery: cat. nos.70,76; Worthing Museum and Art Gallery: cat. no.18; Worthing Museum and Art Gallery / David Nicholls Photography: cat. nos.3, 74; York City Art Gallery (bequeathed by John Burton, 1882): cat. no.6.

Essay: Board of Trustees of the National Museums and Galleries on Merseyside (Lady Lever Art Gallery, Port Sunlight): p.13; Board of Trustees of the National Museums and Galleries on Merseyside (Walker Art Gallery, Liverpool): p.8; © Manchester City Art Galleries: p.9; © Tate Gallery, London: p.10 (below); The Fitzwilliam Museum Cambridge: p.12; The Museum of London: p.10 (top).